HOMAGE
TO MARC CHAGALL

When the Greek bard cries out "woe is me, woe is me", these simple words body forth a poetic reality. Such is the magic of Chagall: a shower of pyrotechnics erupts from two brush-strokes which would have lain inert under any other painter's hand. Of course, this observation also applies to Picasso, the Spaniard, his senior by several years, but who is linked to Chagall as tightly as the east face of an ancient stele is to its west face. Yet while Picasso intellectualizes everything, Chagall de-intellectualizes everything, as was evinced by his brief Cubist period. The one reduces everything to idea, the other to feeling, and yet the elder can no more be regarded as a philosopher than the younger as a sensualist.

For, in the words of Stendhal, both consider art as a matter of sensibility; yet sensibility is always a product of culture: Picasso and Chagall embody two cultures which, though apparently contradictory, actually interpenetrate and which, throughout the twentieth century have been like two great Empires sharing the boundless world of art.

Great poets have celebrated both the "Malagueño" and he who was once called the Master of Vitebsk, the little town where he was born. I felt it was important to recall some of the most beautiful poems inspired by Chagall's world. However, this homage is primarily addressed to the painter. For Chagall is essentially a painter and his poetry flows forth from his paintings the way sap flows forth from a tree. Form is born of color and subsequently engenders the poetry and the music of the work.

Chagall's message, poetic though it may be, is above all a painter's message. It is through him and his splendid work that young painters, after the crisis of recent years, are now rediscovering painting. During the deluge of the sixties, his painting was as precious as an ark for the preservation of human values; for this reason it deserves all our gratitude, and it was that gratitude that inspired this homage.

SAN LAZZARO

I have borrowed the articles by Camille Bourniquel, Dora Vallier, Jacques Thirion and myself from past issues of XXᵉ Siècle. All the others were written especially for this issue.

3

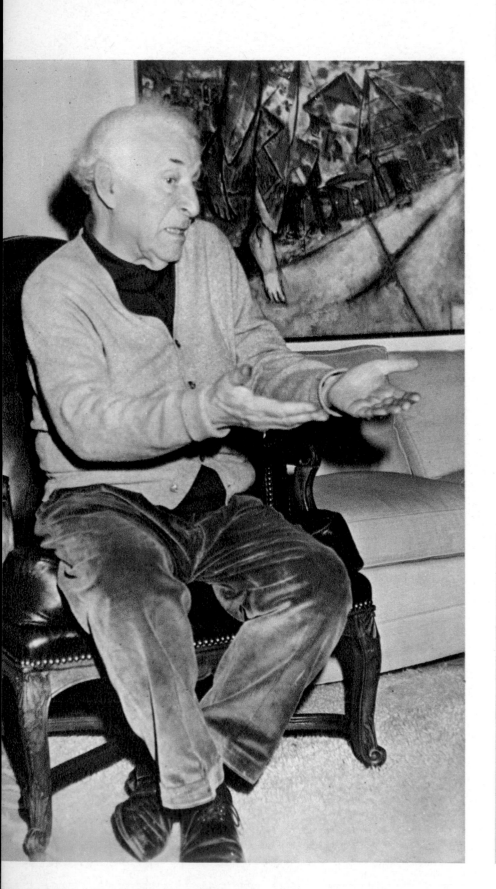

POUR MA

Je me mis à pleurer en me so
Et toi tu me montres un viole
Ce petit tableau où il y a une
Un jour fait de morceaux
Où je m'en allais à la campag
Cheminée tenant sa chienne
Il n'y en a plus tu n'as plus t
La cheminée fume loin de m
La chienne aboie contre les li
La veilleuse est consumée
Sur la robe ont chu des pétal
Deux anneaux d'or près des s
Au soleil se sont allumés
Mais tes cheveux sont le trol
A travers l'Europe vêtue de

(*Rotsage*)

And now if I am asked: "V
answer: "Precisely because h
related to the naive and sub
of La Fontaine.

> "In a new langage h
> "Made brother wolf
> "I've gone further s
> "In my paintings h
> "Are there any who

The enchantment of La Font

4

CHAGALL

. . . .

e vos enfances
table
'a rappelé le jour
unes bleus verts et rouges
e charmante

rliton
cettes russes

multicolores

G. Apollinaire

you chosen Chagall?" I will
s seem close and in a sense
tic and fantastic aesthetics

rother lamb reply.
d plant
conversant
s not enchant?"

enchantment of Chagall!

Ambroise Vollard

ATELIER

. . . .

Des cosaques le Christ un soleil en décomposition
Des toits
Des somnambules des chèvres
Un lycanthrope
Pétrus Borel
La folie l'hiver
Un génie fendu comme une pêche
Lautréamont
Chagall

BLAISE CENDRARS

(Dix-neuf poèmes élastiques)

6

PORTRAIT

. . . .

Il prend une église et peint avec une église

Il prend une vache et peint avec une vache

avec une sardine

avec des têtes, des mains, des couteaux.

Il peint avec un nerf de bœuf...

Le Christ c'est lui

Il a passé son enfance sur la Croix

Il se suicide tous les jours.

BLAISE CENDRARS

A MARC CHAGALL

Ane ou vache coq ou cheval
Jusqu'à la peau d'un violon
Homme chanteur un seul oiseau
Danseur agile avec sa femme

Couple trempé dans son printemps

L'or de l'herbe le plomb du ciel
Séparés par des flammes bleues
De la santé de la rosée
Le sang s'irise le cœur tinte

Un couple le premier reflet

Et dans un souterrain de neige
La vigne opulente dessine
Un visage aux lèvres de lune
Qui n'a jamais dormi la nuit

(Voir)   PAUL ELUARD

CANZONETTA

Sul tetto la vacca
Allatta il vitello
E sogna la donna
Che la munge:
Sogna la forma
Della rozza mano
Come la foglia
A cinque punte.
Cresce in cielo
Avena e frumento,
Cresce il miglio
Nel firmamento.
Sale il rabbino
Sul tetto del ghetto.
Defunti passano
Senza la testa
Nella luna della steppa.

RAFFAELE CARRIERI

THE POETS THEMSELVES WERE DEEPLY

For a long time one serious failing at the roots of those movements—Dada, Surrealism—which were to achieve the fusion of poetry and visual arts consisted in underating the importance of Chagall. Yet the poets themselves were deeply indebted to him—Apollinaire for his "Across Europe", possibly the freest poem of this century, and Cendrars for the "Transiberian"; even Maiakosky and Essenine echo to him in their most convulsive moments. The poet's resistance came later; it was based on the suspicion, no doubt party justified, that Chagall had turned mystic (and in the twenties and thirties any such suspicion brought an automatic and final condemnation). Today it is possible to situate Chagall's work more fairly. His complete lyrical explosion dates from 1911. It marked the triumphal appearance, through his work and no other, of the metaphore in modern painting. In order to consummate that shuffling of the spacial plane which Rimbaud had prepared us for many years earlier, and, at the same time, free objects from the law of gravity, tear down the barriers of the elements and kingdoms, in Chagall's work the metaphore immediately found a visual support in the hypnogogical image and in the eidetic (or aesthesiac) image, which only later came to be endowed with the characteristics that Chagall had bestowed upon it. No work was ever so resolutely magical: its splendid prismatic colors sweep away and transfigure the torment of today and at the same time preserve the age-old spirit of ingenuity in expressing everything which proclaims the pleasure principal: flowers and expressions of love.

ANDRÉ BRETON *(1945)*

Marc Chagall and the architect of the new Metropolitan Opera House, Wallace K. Harrison.

Marc Chagall
and the love of the cosmos

A few of Chagall's remarks

During the hundreds and thousands of years that have preceded us it was much easier morally for a man to live. He had a moral foundation of one kind or another, very deeply embedded, fitting exactly into his conception of life...

Yet with the passing of the years, increasingly, those older conceptions have revealed their impotence to animate human beings and fill their inner lives, to give them the strength they need, not only for creative work but simply to live.

The more audaciously man has freed himself from his so-called chains, the more he feels alone, lost in the multitude, the prisoner of his destiny.

God, perspective, color, the Bible, form, lines, traditions, the so-called humanisms, love, caring, the family, the school, education, the prophets, and Christ Himself have fallen to pieces...

Perhaps I too at times have been beset by doubts. I painted pictures upside down. I cut off heads and hacked my subjects to bits, left floating in the air in my pictures.

In the course of recent years, I have often spoken of the so-called chemistry of authentic color, and of matter, as providing the measure of authenticity. An especially sharp eye can recognize that an authentic color, like authentic matter, inevitably contains all possible techniques. It has also a moral and a philosophical content.

If there is a moral crisis, it is a crisis of color, of matter, of blood and its parts, of words and sounds, and all the rest of the elements with which one constructs a work of art as well as a life. For even if a canvas is covered with mountains of color, whether or not it is possible to distinguish an object—even if there are lots of words and sounds—these do not necessarily make the work authentic.

I should repeat that it is not a new conception of the world, it is nothing literary or symbolic that brings about this change. It is blood itself, a certain chemical process in nature, in things, and even in human awareness. This new authenticity is seen in all sides of life.

She is born and lives and is sustained by love and by a genuine simplicity, like nature itself; she cannot endure wickedness, nor hatred, nor indifference.

In fact, in this epoch, which is marked by a continual weakening in the intensity of religious belief—into the causes for which I do not care to enter—we cannot fail to see how, during the same period, the art of the nineteenth and twentieth centuries appears as a feeble reflection of scientific discoveries. Whereas, up to and including the epoch of the Renaissance, art reflected the religious spirit, or at least illustrated the intense religious feeling of the times. I cannot refrain from saying that so-called scientific art, or the art of pleasure-seeking, like that of cooking, is not a vital value. It can, little by little, fade away.

They say that a good man may be a bad artist. But he isn't and will never be an artist who is not a great and therefore a "good" man.

Changes in the social order, as in Art, are perhaps more trust-worthy if they come from our soul as well as from our intelligence. If men would read more deeply the words of the prophets, they could find in them some keys to life.

It is childish to repeat the truth, which has been known so long: in all its aspects the world can be saved only by love. Without love, it will die little by little.

If the theoretical and scientific sources of art and of life of which I have spoken could be subordinated to love, their results might become valid and more just. In connection with Art I have often spoken of the color which is Love.

These « Commentaries » of Chagall, as well as the replies of Mircea Eliade, have been taken from the brochure published by John Neef, with the authorization of the authors, on behalf of the Center for Human Understanding of the University of Chicago, on the occasion of the « meeting » between Chagall and some of his American friends from 2nd to 4th May, 1963, in Washington.

MARC CHAGALL. One of the twelve stained-glass windows in Jerusalem. Dan. September 1960-May 1961.

Marc Chagall and the love of the cosmos

by Mircea Eliade

"Why have we become so anxious in recent times?" Chagall asks himself. And he sees the chief cause of our collective anxiety in the disintegration of the values which have guided western societies for two thousand years [*a disintegration to which Bourbon Busset has also drawn our attention*]. This process of disintegration has taken many forms. Naturally, Chagall, who is above all a painter, observes the disintegration of traditional values mainly in the recent history of painting. And in that sphere obviously we are witnessing artistic experiments which aim to explode and to destroy the traditional plastic universe.

This is not the place to discuss the causes and profound significance of this will to destroy. Chagall himself recognizes in his declaration that during a certain phase of his career he was tempted, like others, to destroy the "natural" cosmos and replace it with a topsy-turvy world in which he cut off the heads of his subjects to leave them floating in the air. But, what is most rare in our time, Chagall resisted the temptation to demolish altogether the world of his masters and his ancestors.

Perhaps alone among the great masters who

are still alive, Chagall has not succumbed to the general fascination which slaughter has for our contemporaries. Even when he distorts and paints objects upside down, he never really wanted to build another world from scratch. Even in his distortions, there is a love of the "natural" cosmos, expressed especially in the ways he creates his animals.

Yet his refusal to follow the experiments of the cubists and their successors has not been accompanied by an acceptance of any traditional artistic universe, such as, for example, naturalism, romanticism, or impressionism. In refusing to transform living Nature into abstract forms and geometrical spheres, he has not yielded either to the tendency of some of his predecessors to deprive the cosmos of its holy aura in search of the realistic. [*Did not Paul Valéry once suggest that the character of an artist is revealed "by the nature of his refusals"? Chagall has made the right refusals.*]

He has done more. For him the sacred has not been discredited; on the contrary, he has rediscovered the mystery and the holiness of Nature. This is one of the most characteristic traits of

MARC CHAGALL. The ceiling of the Opera. Detail: Tribute to Mussorgsky.

his genius. Nature as studied by the scientists and reproduced by the photographers doesn't interest him. The Nature created by Chagall is primeval and maternal—a place where man, the animal, and the angel live together peacefully under the eye of God, or beneath a great moon such as appeared when the world was first created. For Chagall the archetype of the animal is the donkey—and it is well known that the donkey is *par excellence* the animal of the Messiah.

Chagall's Nature is rich in images and symbols of Paradise. In fact, the friendship between man and the animal world is a paradisiacal symptom— and Chagall loves to illustrate this friendship by the omnipresence of the donkey. We know that before the Fall, man lived in peace with the animals and understood their language. It was only after he was expelled from Paradise that Adam became the animals' enemy and forgot their language. And so we may say that the Nature of Chagall is transfigured by memory of and nostalgia for Paradise. The engaged couple which reappears in his paintings, the angels who float about the villages, are also paradisiacal images.

Chagall's world, this maternal and primeval Nature, inhabited by engaged couples, donkeys, and angels, is the mythological and sacred world of childhood. We are less in the presence of a nostalgic memory than of a past revisited and re-created. The mystery of the world is revealed in childhood, but is generally forgotten afterwards. For maturity abolishes mystery, and removes the holy from the cosmos and from human existence. Chagall has known how to recapture these revelations of childhood. They are most certainly of a religious order—even though the artist is not always conscious of this fact.

That is why the work of Chagall has such a great importance for us. Chagall takes his place among the very few contemporary artists who have recovered the holiness that is present in the world and in human life. Thereby he takes his place among the few who have re-discovered happiness. Such happiness has been lost by almost the entire western intelligentsia following this past half-century of crisis and torment. The work of Chagall shows us that it can be recovered.

MIRCEA ELIADE

MARC CHAGALL. Detail from one of the two murals of the Metropolitan Opera House, New York. 1966.

14

MARC CHAGALL. Original Lithograph for XXᵉ siècle. 1969.

MARC CHAGALL. Self-portrait With Seven Fingers. 1911. 50⅜ x 42⅛ in. Stedelijk Museum, Amsterdam.

The master of
the Imaginary

by   Camille   Bourniquel

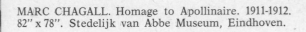

Such as Marc Chagall was on his arrival in Paris in 1911, when he worked in a studio at La Ruche, so he is today. Between the paintings he displayed at the Salon des Indépendants that year in the cubists' gallery, and the ceiling of the Opéra, the stained-glass windows of Metz and Jerusalem, there is, of course, an evolution, a discovery of light and color, a plastic fulfilment, but the vision itself has not changed. There are still the same accessories, the same privileged actors, the same fusion of disparate elements, the same "total lyric explosion", to use the words of André Breton. A world springing from the unknown more than half a century ago and which, throughout so much tragedy, so many rents, has retained its youth, its ascendant vitality, its faith, its ambiguity. A world that would not exist without those trajectories, those levitations, and that seems to have been born already complete like an earlier dream, without hesitations or alterations, with its celestial menagerie, its fluidic bouquets, its exalted couples floating above roof-tops and pursuing the curve of meteors.

There is a Chagall phenomenon—I was going to write a Chagall *mystery*: the very presence of this unusual work situated in the heart of our era but not resembling it, rebellious to appearances, having nothing to do with disputes between schools and purely formal research—perhaps anachronistic... like all prophecies—blending the end and the beginning in a single symbol: duration.

It is this presence—this presence as timeless as everything that helps us to conjure up the platitudes of our time, above all technical and incapable of transposing the imaginary into

---

For the illustration of Camille Bourniquel's article we have preferred to forgo the usual chronological order to present the themes dear to Chagall: gravity, work, celebrations, the "crystallization of childhood memories", but also forebodings and anxiety over coming events: war, racial persecution, themes already found in his works of 1911 and even before the artist left Russia.

MARC CHAGALL. Study for Homage to Apollinaire. 1912. Gouache. 9½" x 8". Berggruen Collection, Paris.

MARC CHAGALL. Self-portrait in yellow, 1914. 16½" x 28". Ilya Ehrenbourg Collection, Moscow.

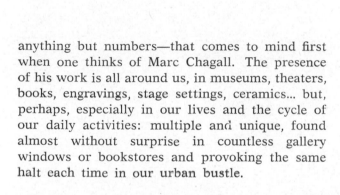

MARC CHAGALL. The Pregnant Woman, 1912-1913. 84½″ x 45″.
Stedelijk Museum, Amsterdam.

anything but numbers—that comes to mind first when one thinks of Marc Chagall. The presence of his work is all around us, in museums, theaters, books, engravings, stage settings, ceramics... but, perhaps, especially in our lives and the cycle of our daily activities: multiple and unique, found almost without surprise in countless gallery windows or bookstores and provoking the same halt each time in our urban bustle.

Time has not touched it; it has kept that almost fairy-like freshness of some countries where we might have often wished to visit and travel, far from the usual frontiers. Chagall has a totally personal way of belonging to his time: he makes it fall into a sort of sleepless dream. He has always refused to take part in aesthetic disputes and to define himself through manifestoes—which has most certainly contributed to the absence of his works in certain superficial chronologies on twentieth century art—but life has put itself in his hands. A life that has kept the sense of unforeseeable élans, of diverse solutions and sudden mutations, marked, it would seem, by the irony of a demiurge amusing himself by upsetting natural laws, mixing up species and kingdoms, and extending to the limits of the absurd the variations of possibilities.

Chagall was, perhaps, the first expressionist. In any case, he far preceded Dadaism and sur-

MARC CHAGALL. Detail of The Pregnant Woman.

MARC CHAGALL. Above Vitesbk, 1914. 27½″ x 35½″.
A. and S. Zacks Collection, Toronto.

MARC CHAGALL. The Blue Violin-player. 1937. 32⅛ x 24¾ in.

18

realism; nor did he wait for psychoanalysis to discover the unconscious mind. Perhaps also, sensing the menace hanging over Europe that was to take definite form between the two wars, he was a Kafka before Kafka and, along with the latter, the most authentic prophet.

For Chagall to exist in his time and yet remain timeless, there must be an eternity promised to man, that he come from a past not devoid of sense and that he direct himself towards something other than a progress that is measurable and already established by statistics and prospectives. Chagall resembles us only in what there is of most intemporal, most mysterious in each of us: that hope to give the world other laws than those that govern it; that hope that dreams of escaping from the existential framework by destroying the poorness of previsions and calculations. Invention, for him, is the exact opposite of logic and of a rule accepted once and for all. What he invents has always freed him from standard techniques and, today as yesterday, from the petrifying experiments of doctrinarians who lock creative genius in geometry or abstract reckonings. Not that he has remained apart from these experiments: all the important trends in modern art have passed through his work without, for as much, becoming the key. There was certainly, as the art critics tell us, a *fauve* Chagall, a cubist Chagall, an expressionist Chagall, a surrealist Chagall. Thus, every period can claim him for the list of their originators—he himself has remained true to his own style and its source sprang from elsewhere.

Nothing, in this respect, seems more conclusive

MARC CHAGALL. The Flying Horse. 1948. 51" x 27½". Abrams Collection, New York.

MARC CHAGALL. The Green Night. Gouache. 1948. Jardot Collection.

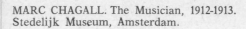

than his *Homage to Apollinaire* (1911), in which the geometric network—diagonals and circles—inscribes the monumental mythical, two-headed figure without breaking its linear unity or its verticality. This figure, which escapes the disjunction of form, with its complementary harmonies of clever geometry (of which Chagall was perfectly capable; consider another work of the same period: *The Poet or Half Past Three*), is rather more reminiscent of the enigma posed by certain alchemic illustrations in which the Uralian creatures of William Blake still carry the weight of the world on their shoulders and sweep away the shadows before them. Yet, even in that moment when he had just come in contact with the School of Paris artists, Chagall never stopped belonging to himself. *To Russia to Donkeys and to Others* and *I and My Village* are contemporary proofs and one could see in them a sort of crystallization of his childhood memories. In any case, this great mythical figure implies no renouncement and therein lies the least servile homage that, through Apollinaire, has ever been paid to cubism.

In truth, pure research and rational organization—Delaunay or Malevitch—that proud *satisfecit* that so many artist permit themselves in measured doses and harmonious proportions, have never been enough to satisfy his instinct. He must have his Russian land; he must have Vitebsk, Paris, the French landscape, Greece, Palestine, Vence and then Vitebsk again. He needs a reality directly and, occasionally, naïvely observed to nourish his unrealism. Even the angel who came to him and whom he painted while he was making his own portrait, that angel he claims to have *truly* seen.

But Chagall knows too that unrealism has meaning only if it leads us towards a less discernable reality; that any form of art that is not a transcendent interrogation is apt to be only a simple play of mirrors. And it is certainly this that distinguishes him from so many other artists who have sought in symbolism and dream images only an artificial liberty and a cheap fantastic.

His choice is obvious. Adventure for him is of a spiritual order—even mystic, that word doesn't frighten him. His strangely weightless world is not an empty world devoid of sense and finality like those of Beckett or Ionesco. Objects can suddenly assume a disproportionate place, and man can exchange his head for that of an animal; derision is not total; the spirit is not driven out of its dwelling by those monstrous proliferations and man does not have to fade into the background before chairs and rhinoceros as is the

case with our modern tragedians of the absurd and senseless.

Whether he illustrates Gogol or Longus, Stravinsky or Ravel, La Fontaine, Mozart or the Prophets, the passage from reality to dream is scarcely noticeable in his work. There is not a moment in Chagall's work when it suddenly plunges into the fantastic and when he must tug on our sleeve to remind us that we are floating in a balloon. The fantastic is the very essence and *raison d'être* of the work. It is less a question of symbols than of an unveiled reality set before our eyes. Chagall knows that reason is often an obstacle to knowledge of the being and the world. This confusion of appearances that can perplex us carries us beyond the illusions that it creates before our eyes. The visionary does not hem himself in here in enigmas and phantasms. His creatures are not mere puppets or robots. These hybrid beings cannot be wound up like toys: they lead their own lives, are fragments of energy, symbols of the spirit which forever passes through

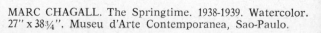

MARC CHAGALL. The Accordionist. 1949. 33½" x 22½.
Perls Gallery, New York.

matter and tricks logic. What counts here is not
that donkeys fly, that roosters become gigantic
canopies, that rabbis are green or red or blue
like the seraphim in some apocalyptic vision, but
that these infractions of natural laws, this il-
legality of form bring forth for us the light of
the being in the heart of these mutations. The
fantastic, or rather the imaginary, in Chagall's
work is a form of knowledge, a gesture to embrace
the world in its totality.

We are at the antipodes of gratuitousness, facing evidence so profound and yet so natural that
it seems almost useless to seek its sources and
models.

> *My only country*
> *Is there where my soul dwells.*
> *I enter without passport*
> *As if going home.*

Let us remember this affirmation. There is no
intentional delirium, ecstasy or anguished discovery of abysses, but a free and open entrance
into that mysterious domain that is the meeting
place of the closest reality and transcendance,
naïvety and illumination. This partially dual
universe, as Chagall himself reminds us, was that
of Douanier Rousseau: "It is the greatest miracle.
He had need of fairy tales, nude women in forests
and exotic plants. Here is a painter of the people
and for the people. More innocent, more grandiose
than Courbet or Seurat." In Chagall's paintings,
the impatience of the mind demands other ex-
tensions beyond the visible. Aragon was right in
saying, *"You paint the gravity whereby the body
is made soul."* The soul, there is the key word
and the final goal of this whole quest. Here the
artist recaptures the old Slav and Jewish heritage:
nothing in his life has made him budge one inch

MARC CHAGALL. The
Bear with a Violin.
Stage setting for the
Aleko Ballet. Museum of
Modern Art, New York.

MARC CHAGALL. The Fall of the Angel. 1923-33-47. 58½" x 58¾". Museum of Basel.

from these certitudes. He knows how to hide methodical concern, exemplary diligence (repitition of the same themes, preparatory studies and sketches, reconstitutions of his lost paintings) under the guise of the freest fantasy, naïvety and even improvisation and stays in this spiritual trend that remains almost constantly ambiguous and out of balance beneath irony and paradox. Here, the symbol is only a marker, a sign on that road to knowledge. Everything brings us back to that vision which we gradually discover as we study the whole of his work, the depth, the seriousness and the extraordinary coherence.

"Come back, you're famous and Vollard is waiting for you," wrote Blaise Cendrars to Chagall in Berlin in 1922 when the artist had just left Russia for the second and last time. Few works have known such quick success in the world of art. Few men have had such a predestination.

That is a fact that greatly exceeds the usual data found in a biography. Chagall possesses an energy, a power of persuasion, a communicative and emotional force that are almost impossible to ignore. One has the impression that he has always existed: that before Chagall there was already a Chagall and that he will always be here, flitting over frontiers, scrambling all the pasts of a Europe that, through him, has rediscovered the old Biblical sources and the most ancient revelations.

Chagall feels himself to be heir to a tradition more mystic than humanist, and although that tradition is basically Judaic, his personal temperament urges him towards a syncretism. "I remember my distant ancestor who painted in the Mohilev synagogue." But, at the same time, Christian art began to fascinate him even in his youth, and especially the gallery of icons in the

23

MARC CHAGALL. The Acrobat. 1914. 16½" x 13".
Albright-Knox Gallery, Buffalod, New York.

MARC CHAGALL. The Circus. 1927. Gouache.
Vollard Collection.

Museum of Alexander III in Saint Petersburg.
He calls Roublev "our Cimabue", thus confirming
from the beginning his debt to those other images
whose mysterious kinship he tries to evaluate.
"My heart became calm before the icons." Never
has he obeyed the law that banishes the representation of the human figure. It has often
been claimed that the importance of animals in
his paintings is a means of avoiding this forbidden iconoclasm: I cannot accept this theory, for
to depict the common man, his neighbors and
himself remains one of those vital needs of which
he has never deprived himself. Even if his
Christs, according to some authorities, seem to
fit a more Jewish than Christian conception, He
is as central and essential in his work as He was
in Dostoevski's and so many other Russians
haunted, they too, by the idea of human misery
and redemption.

Such a fusion—must it be pointed out?—does
not take place on a theological level but on a
spiritual one. A recent pope reminded us that
spiritually we are all Semites. A certain religious
ambivalence in Chagall seems to illustrate this
statement. Furthermore, one realizes very quickly
that this syncretism is identified with an instinc-

MARC CHAGALL. The Horsewoman. 1927. 39½" x 32.
National Gallery, Prag.

MARC CHAGALL. Feast Day or the Rabbi in Yellow. Detail. 1914. 39⅜ x 31⅝ in. Kunstsammlung Nordrhein-Westfalen, Düsseldorf.

MARC CHAGALL. To Russia, to Donkeys and Others. Detail. 1911. 61¾ x 48 in. Musée National d'Art Moderne, Paris.

MARC CHAGALL. Lovers Above the Town. Detail. 1917. 61⅜ x 83⅝ in. Tretiakoff Gallery, Moscow. (*Photo Giraudon, Paris*).

MARC CHAGALL. Time Has No Boundaries. 1930-39. 40½ x 32⅝ in. Museum of Modern Art, New York.

MARC CHAGALL. Three Acrobats. 1959. 39 x 26 in. Property of the Artist.

MARC CHAGALL. The Gray House. 1917. 26¾" x 29. Pechère Collection, Brussels.

tive need that urges him to join the sources of his inspiration in a single creative movement. "My poetry is unexpected, Oriental, suspended between China and Europe," he said, thus opening even larger horizons. He has a need of that absence of intellectual, historical and religious frontiers to encompass in a single vision realism and enchantment, a certain ritual fidelity (The Tables of the Law, the seven-branch candelabrum, the celebrations in the Jewish calendar...) and a pantheism (numerous nudes, his late discovery of Greece...); on the one hand, adoration and, on the other, a fundamental disrespect that alone permits a dialogue with God.

This fusion is not total. As in any baroque work, the gamut of possibilities remains essential.

Metamorphosis passes through this universe, as in Kafka's, and it often seems that man has trouble establishing his privilege in the midst of those gravitations of which he is not necessarily the center. As in Shakespeare, reality is crossed with fairy tale. The angel mixes with the beast, the musician becomes the 'cello, the donkey's profile blends with that of the artist.

For those who see in this jumble of unusual objects passing through a strange and drifting cosmos only caprices of the imagination, happy or gloomy humor, zoomorphic deformations, tricks and facileness, Chagall reminds us that all painting—and his, in particular—is a tragic language, often marked by blood and tears, in any case, for him by dramas he has experienced

30

MARC CHAGALL. The Lights of
the Wedding. 1945. 48⅜ x 47¼ in.

MARC CHAGALL.
The Wedding. 1917.
39⅜ x 46⅞ in.
Tretiakoff Gallery,
Moscow.

MAR CHAGALL. The Wedding. 1910. 38½" x 74". The artist's collection.

or witnessed: the Russian revolution, a double rootedness and, finally, the Germans' massacres of eastern European Jewish communities. It is possible that nothing remains today of the Vitebsk that he knew as a child, returned to during the Lenin period where he married Bella and founded an academy for the working classes in those days of famine and denunciations: the image, in any case, remains primordial and has colored his whole life. That retrospective tenderness for those streets, those houses "destroyed with infancy" and its "inhabitants wandering about in the air," those artisans, those woodcutters, those fishermen in the Dvina, those old men, those rabbis, those fiddlers in front of isbas find other

justification than the nostalgia of an exile, another setting than picturesqueness. Something unusual is added to the picturesqueness, mixing animals and men, the synagogue and the street, weddings and funerals: a masked menace, the flames of burning towns and pogroms. It is in that presentiment of inevitable tragedy hanging over that little world where his fantasy has given itself free rein that gives the vision of something so poignant and so human. "Sometimes there stood before me a figure so tragic and so old that it looked more like an angel." A very revealing phrase: misery, instead of immobilizing appearances, encourages a sort of gliding towards the invisible. Chagall has always seen in those old

MARC CHAGALL. Marriage with Fish. 1955-56. Maeght Gallery.

MARC CHAGALL. Midsummer Night's Dream. 1939. Museum of Grenoble.

MARC CHAGALL. I and the Village. 1914. 75½" x 61". Detail. Museum of Modern Art, New York.

MARC CHAGALL. I and the Village.

men in prayer, those humble and menaced men, the true witnesses of eternity.

That distant, premonitory vision has not lessened his liking for life and creatures, for present and fleeting things. Chagall has an optimism that can accept appearances and transitory things. Above all, there is in him a man who has studied himself a great deal; I might even say chosen and loved himself such as God made him. From this springs the series of self-portraits marking his work and making him his own principal interpreter. He himself seems to have wished to establish and bequeath the entire geneology of his own faces from the Apollo of Vitebsk. He loved his youth, and the companionship of the angel of the unusual has not added a wrinkle of bitterness to his features.

Thus, he marks his presence in an imaginary universe ordered by the law of multiple and constant mutations. It is not mere self-complacency, for this liking for oneself is almost immediately diversified and balanced by the presence and mythology of the couple. Chagall does not remain in that obsessive phase where his own face fascinates the artist more than any other

33

Detail of "The Wedding".

34

MARC CHAGALL. The Cattle-dealer. 1912. 39⅜ x 77⅞ in. Basle Museum.

MARC CHAGALL. The Stable. 1917. 18½ x 24⅛ in. Belmont Binningen Coll., Basle.

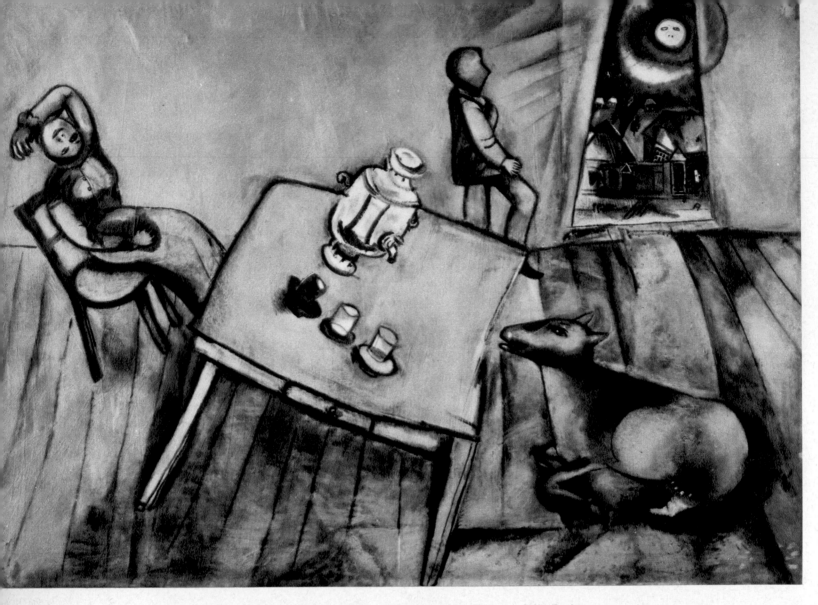

MARC CHAGALL. The Yellow Room. 1912. 32⅝ x 43⅛ in. Paul Hänggi Coll., Basle.

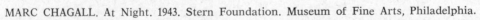

MARC CHAGALL. At Night. 1943. Stern Foundation. Museum of Fine Arts, Philadelphia.

MARC CHAGALL. The Calvary. 1912. 67¾ x 77 in. Museum of Modern Art, New York.

MARC CHAGALL. The House With the Green Eye. 1944. 15 x 20⅛ in. Ida Meyer-Chagall Coll., Basle.

MARC CHAGALL. The Dead Man. 1908. 27⅜ x 34¼ in. Private Coll. (*Photo A. Held*).

MARC CHAGALL. The Walk. 1929. 21⅝ x ⅜ in. Private Coll.

MARC CHAGALL. Night in Vence, 1952. 38¼" x 51". Private Collection, Zurich.

enigma and becomes a sign of solitude as was the case of Van Gogh. His ego splits, becomes enthusiastic, and fulfills itself, in a way, in the description of the loved woman. We find the image of Bella, fiancée, wife, mother, in a whole series of portraits, drawings, compositions that, beginning with an occasional element—black gloves, a birthday bouquet, a carnation, a shawl, a white collar—recounts, until her death in 1942, a long and splendid poem of an inseparable presence in Chagall's destiny.

Perhaps there has not existed in all of the history of art an artist who has transposed in such a constant way his private life and consecrated it to the apotheosis of the couple. His admirable *Lovers above Vitebsk* (1917) shows us how, from the beginning, this image integrates itself with that imaginary universe and even gives it new dynamic breadth. The theme of his double levitation will be repeated endlessly: Bella appears to play the constant role of mediator and inspirer. In some moments she is the axis of that universe. The famous *Double Portrait with a Glass of Wine* (1918) in which Chagall depicted himself strad-

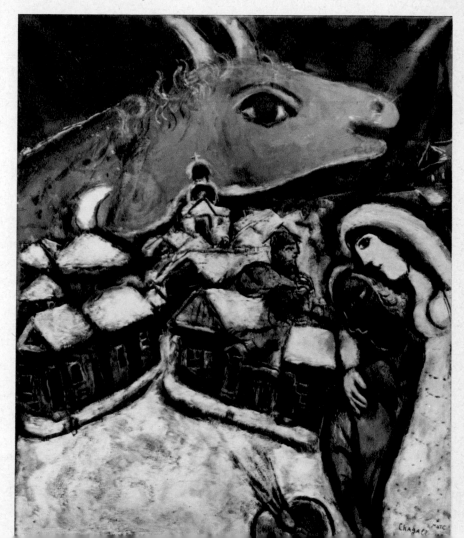

MARC CHAGALL. The Green Night. 1952. Painting 28½" x 23½". Private Collection, Basle.

MARC CHAGALL. The Doors to the Cemetery. 1917. 34½" x 27. Ida Meyer Chagall Collection, Basle.

dling his young wife's shoulders expresses, of course, a joy bordering on intoxication but, above all, the real meaning of the couple. The two of them form a column of which Bella is the foundation of unvarying strength and security and he, Chagall, the dionysiac crowning.

The imagery of happiness involves the same sentimentalism, the same naïvety, the same thematic variations as the memories of Vitebsk or Lyozno. The imaginary has no other stepping stone than this lived reality. From this stems the importance, for Chagall, of the human milieu and emotional and family surroundings. Love and sentiment are not for him mere motivations, simple narrative incidents: they create exaltation, encourage the harmonious liberation of the being freed from that ultimate anxiety, that senselessness: solitude.

MARC CHAGALL. The Burial. 1909. 26⅜ x 53½ in. Antoine Bernheim Coll., Paris.

MARC CHAGALL. The Fire. 1913. 42⅜ x 47¼ in. The Solomon R. Guggenheim Museum, New York.

MARC CHAGALL. The War. 1943. Musée Municipal d'Art Moderne, Paris.

MARC CHAGALL. The Russian Soldier. 1912.
Tempera. 15¾" x 12½".

Nature and landscapes also participate in this exaltation of the consciousness, and if one can speak of a French influence it is much more in this domain than in the ideologies of form that it will be found. Here, an inner illumination joins the visible. Chagall discovered through the years all that attaches him to France, composed of living contrasts, of nuances, where snow does not extinguish light or smother reliefs during six months of winter's white mourning. The necessity of leaving France during the Occupation only made him more conscious of that intimate mixture of Paris and Vitebsk in his mythology. "Absence, war and suffering were necessary for all that to awaken in me and to become the framework of my thoughts and my life. But this is only possible for a person who has retained his roots. To keep the earth on one's roots or to find another earth is a true miracle."

The world has, of course, changed in fifty years in its rhythm and obsessions; Paris is no longer exactly the city that Apollinaire and Blaise Cendrars knew and loved; but Chagall is here among us, not as a survivor of an age but continuing, to the contrary, to make his way between reality and dream, the tragedy of man and the experience of human and divine love.

What strikes me in his most recent large compositions: the ceiling of the Opéra or the

MARC CHAGALL. The Goat Composition. 1917. 15" x 19½". Franz Meyer Collection.

MARC CHAGALL. The Revolution.
Sketch. 1937. 19⅝ x 39⅜ in.
Property of the Artist.

MARC CHAGALL. Detail
of the Revolution: Lenin.

MARC CHAGALL. The Jesse Tree. 1960. 59" x 47¼"
Marcus Diener Collection, Basle.

stained-glass windows depicting the Twelve Tribes of Israel, is Chagall's power to be himself completely in every instant. It is the sovereign ease with which he masters his invention, summoning once more to himself all the astrological figures of his sky, all the symbols of his faith, and moving without apparent effort through the world he created.

Language, poetry, music continue to exchange their powers in this universal metaphor. Perhaps Chagall has never felt a desire to cross the threshold of revelation to choose a permanent style between illumination and wisdom. This unstable equilibrium between two temptations is, perhaps, the last moral of a man who has long meditated on his fate and on that of his fellow men.

I went to talk to him, or rather to see him and listen. He touched the leaf of a plant in front of him and said, "There you are... what counts, what is the most important of all is the texture!" I tried to complete this thought in my own mind. Texture... yes, that which joins depth and surface, the upper and the lower, the beginning and the end, the shimmering and that thing which the hand can grasp and retain.

CAMILLE BOURNIQUEL

MARC CHAGALL. The Newlyweds of the Eiffel Tower.

MARC CHAGALL. The Donkey with the Large Bouquet.
Maeght Gallery, Paris.

47

MARC CHAGALL. Detail of The Newlyweds of the Eiffel Tower. 1928.

MARC CHAGALL. The Creation of Man. Painting. 1956-58. 118⅛ x 76¾ in.

Marc Chagall's biblical message

The song of songs in color

On bequeathing to posterity his "Biblical Message", did Marc Chagall choose? Of course, one can never forget the secular artist, the painter of the "Aleko" curtains, of "The Firebird", of "Daphnis and Cloe" and a hundred other master-pieces, the same works to which, after the Museum of Zurich, the Maeght Foundation in Saint-Paul (France) and the Museum of Toulouse are going to pay homage. It is true that even on finding inspiration in music and love, the artist remains in the "sacred" which Mircea Eliade has defined so well. However, the Biblical world is the "sacred" captured at its source: it flows directly from the Book of Prophets.

Marc Chagall's Biblical world was rediscovered by the men of my generation in their adolescence by leafing through the artistic and literary maga-zines of that time. We recaptured the reality of it in Chagall's work for he had been until then, for the children we were, a pure abstraction like the Earthly Paradise and the Tree of Good and Evil. It is the reality of this sacred but imaginary world that our teachers and parents, unaware of it themselves, would have wished us to be unaware of, too. A world in which the poor, too, like the Greek hero, the slave on the Egyptian bas-relief or the rich adolescents of the Florentine aristo-cracy or bourgeoisie, had a right not only to

MARC CHAGALL. Paradise. Oil. 75 x 115 in.

MARC CHAGALL. Adam and Eve driven from Paradise. Oil. 76 x 113 in.

charity but also to their share of poetry; whatever "poetry" means today.

This race, whose inexorable destiny was forged by Moses and his brother Aaron, what would it have become if it had not been taken out of the still welcoming Egypt where it was already worshipping Pharaoh's gods? It's simple: there would not have been any Prophets and poet kings, no Bible and, thus, no Christ, the end result for us of the crossing of the Red Sea and the Sinai Desert: that Christ child to whom Chagall paid homage in 1912 in the famous painting, belonging to the Museum of Modern Art of New York, whose plastic qualities equal those of Picasso's *Guernica* which is considered one of the masterpieces of that great Spanish painter. I don't know what emotions urged Chagall to paint this picture at a time when the children of Israel still considered Christ as the symbol of the long period of persecution endured through the centuries and whose existence obliged them to remain outlaws, to live in the expectation of returning to Israel.

This Christ is a child, just as in the arms of some Portuguese Virgins, the Christ child is the bearded Christ he was later to be, wearing a crown of thorns and not that ridiculous royal crown in which the Son of God is generally rigged out. It seems to me that in order to understand the sense of Marc Chagall's Biblical message

(which more recently has voluntarily interwoven the Old and New Testaments by painting the stained-glass windows in Jerusalem as well of those for the cathedral of Metz), one must go back to this first example of reconciliation, to which cubism lent its traits.

Why did Marc Chagall paint that picture? I like to think that it was out of love for that image of man, in whom, he too, loving his neighbor as himself, recognized himself, and who had been, like him, before becoming a symbol, a child who astonished adults by his knowledge and intelligence. It was not, however, a personal gesture dictated by his own conscience, since the millenary world from which he sprang and which saw in him its first great painter, did not disapprove of him, did not veil its face like Abraham over Sara's corpse, did not reject him like a renegade from the community. That world understood, approved and admired its painter.

I have just seen in the basement of the Musée National d'Art Moderne in Paris the seventeen paintings to be exhibited in the Louvre in a few weeks. Like many people, I read Eugène Ionesco's article this morning on *the ignoble scoundrels:* "A race is in danger of being destroyed. A race that is not asking for the place of others but only a small place to live in this world... A race

51

MARC CHAGALL. Noah's Ark. Oil. 94 x 93 in.

that has more right to live than any other because it has been the most slandered, persecuted, tortured... The moderation of the reactions of the world's moral conscience fills me with indignation. It has always been so..."

Around 1930, wishing to illustrate the Bible for the publisher Ambroise Vollard, for whom he had already created extraordinary engravings for *Dead Souls* and for La Fontaine's *Fables*, Marc Chagall, accompanied by his wife and his daughter Ida, went to Jerusalem, discovering the land of their ancestors and the sky that opened to submerge the world, with the exception of the wise Noah, his sons and the animals, but also to make the celestial manna, like honey from a hive, fall on the heroes of the great Exodus. This return to Hebraic sources by a native of provincial Russia was obviously an important stage in the artist's life and evolution. However, its importance is entirely different from, for example, Delacroix's trip to the Orient. For Chagall, the pilgrimage to Palestine was not a revelation but a confirmation, for Palestine, its history, its legend has always

dwelled in his heart (where he was also to discover Greece). In his childhood home, in his Vitebsk, he had spoken of and dreamed of the Holy History. Abraham's hand, covering his face beside Sara's mortal remains, was his father's hand; the Prophets were no less familiar to him than the friends of his family, and the animals of the Ark had been his first and only toys. Thus, it was not a reflection of a world gone forever that he discovered in Palestine, but its sky, its light—that light in which the children of Israel purified themselves, like an offering to the Eternal.

Even before setting foot on the land of the Hebrews, Chagall was already considered, and with reason, a great colorist. It was on his return, when we saw the gouaches that he brought back to France, that we discovered that his colors before the trip, in spite of the pleasure they gave us, were still objective, impersonal. He had lacked that sacred fire that he discovered in Palestine, his "chemistry"—that mysterious word that the artist was later to use—subjective, inimi-

MARC CHAGALL. Moses Facing the Burning Bush. Painting. 76¾ x 83⅜ in.

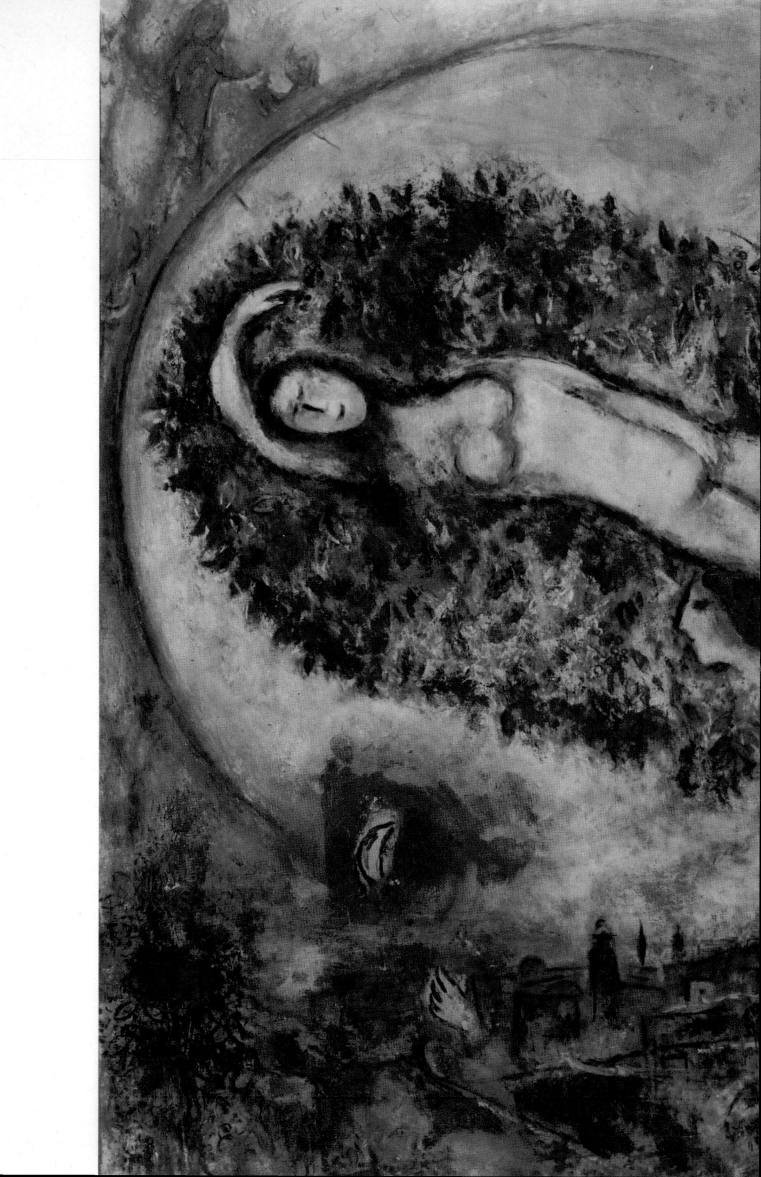

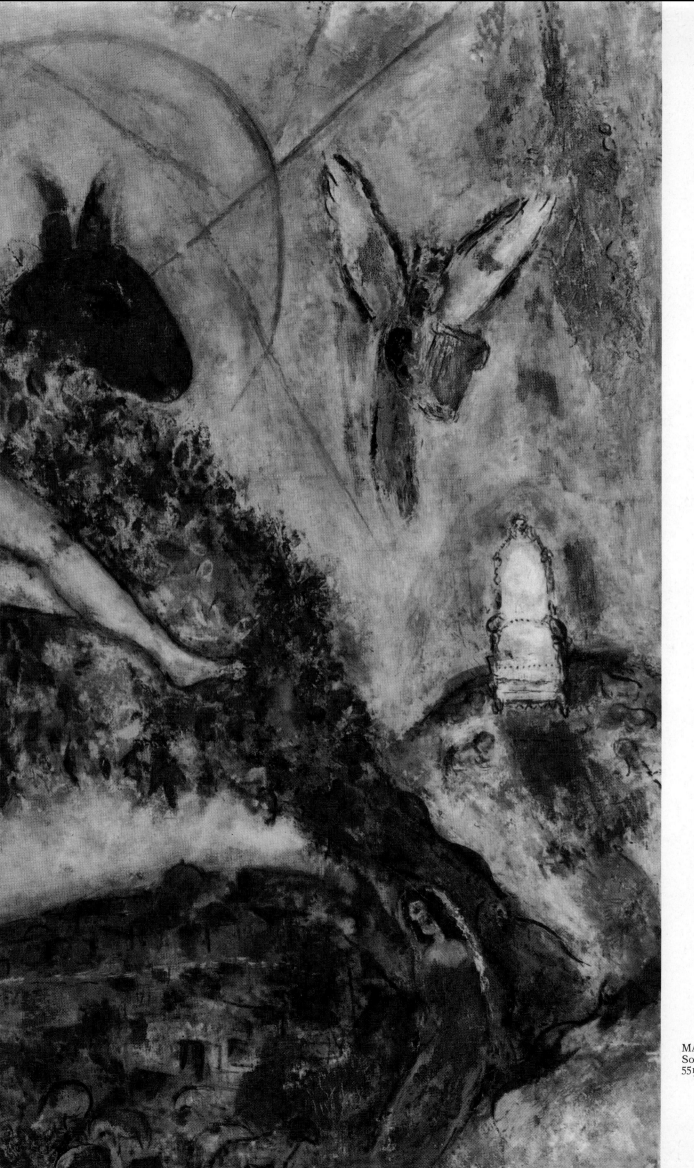

MARC CHAGALL. The Song of Songs. Painting. 1957. 55⅛ x 60⅝ in.

MARC CHAGALL. Jacob's Struggle With the Angel. Painting. 94⅜ x 81⅛ in.

table. Chagall certainly realized the new power of his colors but, modestly, continued to believe that one cannot demand more of a painter's palette than to hold its own with the color of his garden or the bouquets of roses placed by Madame Chagall each day on the living room tables. I agreed with him until the day when, the contrast being too evident, I dared to tell him that he had been misleading me, that "his" red had a luminosity, a gentle fury, a "chemistry" that did not exist in nature's red, and that I really could not put them on the same level. "I'm sorry," he said, looking at me with astonishment and blushing like a child.

That light of Palestine undoubtedly palpitated and sang in his heart like no other light ever had before, but it is in his artistic inner depths that he found the one, the unique that will assure his fame during the centuries to come. It is not a vegetal explosion, it is not possessed of that joy that the artist, in his modesty and in his love of nature, believed he could give it, but the fluidity, the sparkle, the fire of mineral, the purity of precious gems or molten metal. Without speaking of mystic colors, even without the artist's knowledge, that "chemistry" has been modified, has, in a manner of speaking, become inflamed

and purified. Since his first trip to Palestine, it illuminates his canvases like a stained-glass window. And we recapture in front of these seventeen paintings of the "Donation" the same enchantment we felt a few years ago before the twelve stained-glass windows of the Synagogue of Jerusalem: it is the Song of Songs in color.

However, the supreme test for a colorist is black and white and monochrome. Only Matisse knew how to "suggest", like Chagall, the magic of color in his drawings, in certain gouaches and a few paintings without actually using it.

Is this "Biblical Message", thus, a message of poetry? Undoubtedly: just as of Solomon's glorious reign there exists only one beautiful poem of love, the history of Israel—and Christ, too, belongs to the history of Israel—like the bloody tragedy of the Atridae, is nothing more than song where the dramatic rhythm rings with nostalgia in the heart of this great painter and great poet, Marc Chagall, that Mozart of painting. But it is, above all, a message of faith. We tremble these days, dear Ionesco, at the idea that this poetry, this faith may become mere history again, and your indignation at the moderation of our reactions fills our consciences with shame.

Of all the great painters of our time, Chagall alone has not felt the very ephemeral call of actuality. Braque himself at the end of his life

MARC CHAGALL. Noah and the Rainbow. Oil. 82 x 117 in.

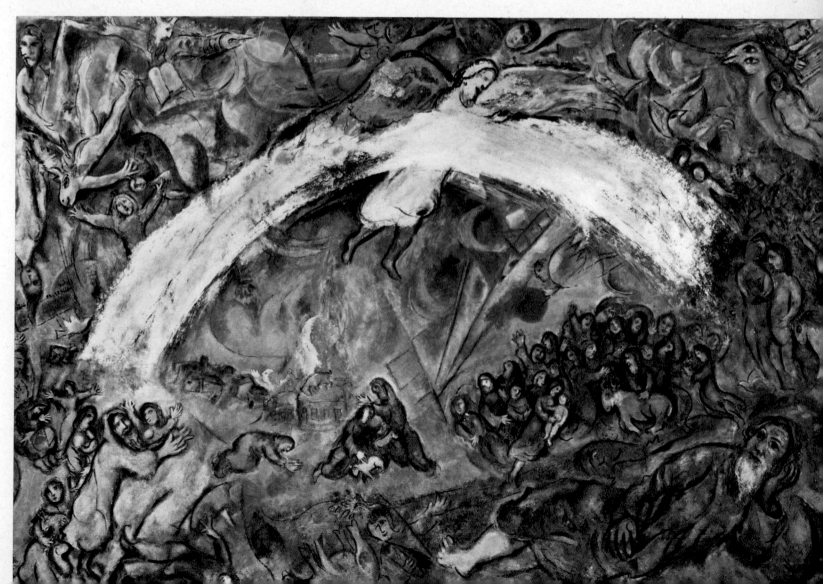

felt obliged to sacrifice quality to quantity and covered his canvases with a thick paste that his brush tilled like a plow. Picasso has occasionally let color flow from his brush like a *tachiste* painter. Chagall, rather than reply to the call of the new "isms", on growing older (an incorrect term, for his youthfulness of spirit and his physical resistance are amazing), seems to be drawn by that of his great elders: it is his manner of growing older without shame that shows his Oriental origins. Like a Chinese sage he is able to love youth—and even with a certain coquetry—while keeping his poetry sheltered from the tumult. I told him one day that Jean-Paul Sartre reproached Titian (whom he called Vecellio, the better to emphasize his scorn) for not having been an "involved" painter. "What?" replied Chagall. "Why, he was "involved" in his painting to the very last drop of his blood."

To the very last drop of his blood: for sixty years Chagall has been "involved", with steady happiness, in his painting, and with a vigor, a freshness, a youthfulness that very few artists, at his age, have experienced.

The painter of Jerusalem's stained-glass windows —that rare proof of today's genius—taught us how important it is to limit each element of a picture by enclosing it in its contour, as if in armor, the better to insert it in the composition, thereby strengthening its unity. In his paintings, on the other hand, all frontiers between heaven and earth, between man and the cosmos, are abolished. Chagall gives way, in his turn, to enchantment. One thinks of the famous lines by Leopardi: "*E il naufragar m'è dolce in questo mare.*" But it would be rash to think that the painter has said everything and given all he has to give. I am convinced, to the contrary, that we can confidently expect a new stage in his evolution which will constitute a happy synthesis of his work.

Will blood flow in Jerusalem? Someone told me this morning that, by way of precaution, the stained-glass windows are being removed, only one of which—the "window" of the Gad tribe—recalls the horrors of war. Chagall has never sung like Jeremiah: "Prepare ye the buckler and shield, and draw near to battle. Harness the horses, and get up, ye horsemen." Over his work only the banner of love is unfurled: love for man and love for painting. In a period when both are brutally shaken, under a thousand pretexts, the artist recaptures in that love "the sacred present in the world"—according to the expression employed by Mircea Eliade in her excellent article. "Thus, he takes his place," she adds "among the human beings who have rediscovered happiness,"—a happiness of which the Western élite have almost lost the sense. For a painter, happiness is, above all, the joy of painting.

May 1967   SAN LAZZARO

MARC CHAGALL. Noah Releasing the Dove. Gouache. 1931.

MARC CHAGALL. Abraham's Sacrifice. Oil.

Chagall and his grand-sons at the opening of the exhibition of his Biblical Message at the Louvre.

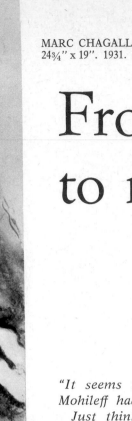

MARC CHAGALL. The Daughters of Lot. Gouache. 24¾" x 19". 1931.

From memories to myth

by Dora Vallier

"It seems to me that my first little rabbi in Mohileff had the greatest influence on me.

Just think, every Saturday, instead of being able to swim in the river, my mother sent me to him to study the Bible...

Day after day, winter and summer, at six in the morning my father got up and went to the synagogue...

It is time for evening prayers. Already night! Blue stars. Violet earth...

MARC CHAGALL. Jacob's Dream. Painting. 76¼" x 109".

MARC CHAGALL. The Striking of the Rock. Painting. 92½" x 91".

Everyone is wailing, crying.

But the stronger men, accustomed to everything, move the women aside and calmly light the candles and, in the midst of silence, begin to pray out loud over the dead man.

The gleam from the yellow candles, the complexion of the man who has just died, the self-assured gestures of the old men, their impassive eyes, convince me and those around me that all is over.

All day long we hear the lamentations of the children singing "The Song of Songs"...

My father, lifting his glass, tells me to go open the door. To open the door at such a late hour! —is it to let the prophet Ilya enter?

A shower of white stars, silvery on the blue velvet background of the sky, penetrates my eyes and my heart.

But where is Ilya and his white chariot?

Perhaps he is still in the courtyard and will come into the house in the guise of a weak old man, of a stoop-shouldered beggar with a sack on his back and carrying a cane.

—Here I am, where is my glass of wine?...
The Day of Pardon.

Slowly, gravely, the Jews unfold their holy veils soaked with tears from a whole day of praying.

Their clothing unfolds like fans.

The murmur of their voices comes through the archway where the doors are sometimes visible, sometimes hidden.

I am suffocating. I do not move.

MARC CHAGALL. Moses receiving the Tables of the Law. Painting. 93½" x 92".

Infinite day. Take me, make me closer to you. Say a word, explain.

All day long I hear 'Amen! Amen!' and I see all of them kneeling.

If You exist, turn me blue, fiery, lunar; hide me with the Thora, do something, God, in our name, in my name!

Our spirit evaporates and beneath the colored windows arms are raised.

Outside, the withered branches of the tall poplars sway peacefully.

In broad daylight small clouds drift by, break, fade away.

Soon the moon, a half-moon, will appear.

The candles are almost burned out and small flames glow today in the innocent air.

Now a candle rises to the moon, now the moon flies down towards our arms.

The road itself pray. The houses cry.

The sky passes in all directions.

My memory is on fire."

In 1930, Chagall proposed to Vollard to illustrate the Bible. Their agreement involved a certain number of engravings for a deluxe edition. Thus, it was on the fringe of his other work. However, once it was undertaken it became the center. Before starting the engravings, Chagall painted a series of gouaches on Biblical themes. He felt

MARC CHAGALL. Abraham Mourning Sara. Gouache. 24½" x 19½".

a need, he explained, (as Franz Meyer tells us in his exemplary book), to find "the color" of the Biblical world—a quest that led him to the very sites of sacred history, and it was only on his return from Palestine that he began his engravings. But when they were completed and finally edited he executed, in 1955 and over a period of several years, seventeen large paintings which represent Biblical scenes. This periplus, as a whole, constitutes the "Biblical Message" that Chagall has just bequeathed to the French Musées Nationaux.

An occasion has become an event. This dilatation of an initial idea that eventually pushed Chagall's work to the foreground took place because, as in every instance of Chagall's work, it was a conquest of the past. And wasn't the road that was to lead the painter back to his origins already traced in the account of his life that he had written well before illustrating the Bible? (1) The true commentary on his works is found in those pages which, placed beside the

---

(1) *Ma vie*. Stock, 1931.

MARC CHAGALL. The Song of Songs. Painting. 58½" x 82½".

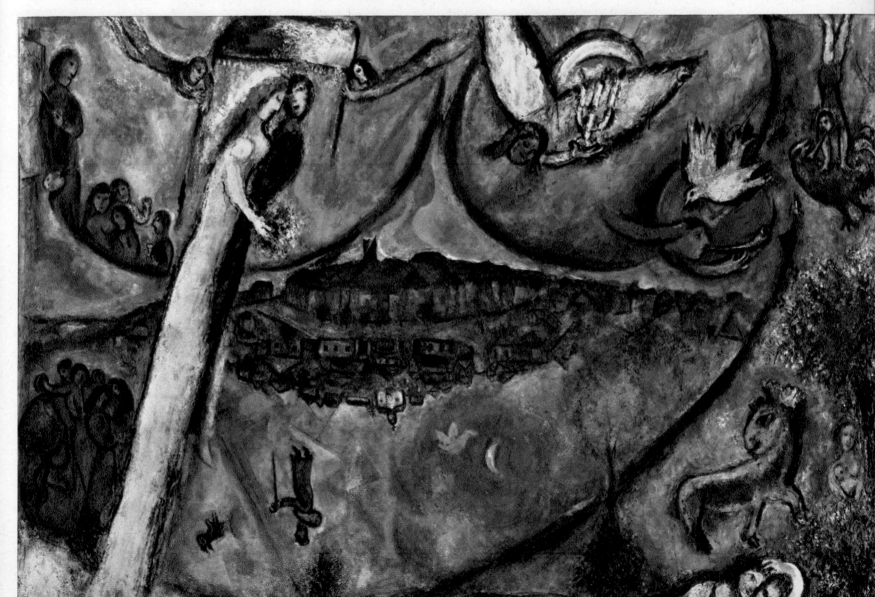

MARC CHAGALL. The Song of Songs. Painting. 58½" x 67¾".

"Biblical Message", illuminate it and, like a shutter, close all around him to preserve the freshness and the secrecy.

Once again Chagall has remained true to himself, and to the very end. The Biblical world, object of his research, urged him in the opposite direction, the unique core of his entire work: his childhood which he was able to recapture from the most distant dimension of childhood—that of the sacred. Distance and closeness, thus intermingled, have exchanged their characteristics: man's fate bound to God has, for Chagall, assumed a familiar aspect. The myth has catalyzed the memory. A daring alchemy that presupposes an unshakable candor. A very personal solution in which the voice of the heart, always preponderant for Chagall, has prevailed.

Verse after verse, Chagall has animated the Bible which interests him right from the creation of man, when the supernatural is already per-

MARC CHAGALL. Moses Spreading the Shadows. Gouache. 24½" x 19¼".

MARC CHAGALL. The Song of Songs. Painting. 59" x 89½".

petuated through nature and when the painter's imagination can, as a consequence, find a foothold in life. "I wasn't seeing the Bible, I was dreaming it," Chagall admits, but in terms of human ex-

perience just as, far from Vitebsk, he dreamed of his city in his paintings with each street, each house, each creature and each thing that he had loved. He confided that "art, consciously and voluntarily fantastic, was foreign to him." Thus, this dream from which the fantastic is absent is none other than memory. Life seen from a distance through a "memory on fire".

From this arises the double action found in the scenes from the Bible. On one hand, the painter makes an act of faith by losing himself in the universal context which he faithfully retraces, (the Marc Chagall shell, however solid, is broken here), but, at the same time, he adds to this context the same fire that inflames his memory. He identifies himself with Man's adventure and relives it as if it were his own, as if it were its very own, for he dreams one and the other in his own way. The particular lends its effigy to the universal and thus becomes enlarged. The memory

MARC CHAGALL. The Israelites Eating the Lamb of the Passover. Gouache. 24½" x 19¼". 1931.

MARC CHAGALL. The Song of Songs. Painting. 58" x 83". 1958.

gives life to the symbol and its own horizon is widened. Chagall passes easily from one Biblical episode to another. Narration has always been his forte. Is not narration inherent in memory? Gestures and Biblical characters come in profusion from his brush. He paints joyously with color of which he demands each time, in his own words, "to be as penetrating as when one walks on a thick carpet": but he does not become exultant until he reaches "The Song of Songs". The victory over fatality, the triumph of love is obviously what touches Chagall the most in the Bible: he did five versions of "The Song of Songs", whereas only one version was sufficient for the other episodes he chose. One cannot imagine an artist more free before such an intimidating sum of meanings. There is no trace, however, of irreverence in his complete rejection of traditional iconography. To the contrary, it is a reconsecration due, undoubtedly, to the profound involvement that guides Chagall and protects him from any sort of conventional imitation. This is the greatest proof of the importance of the stamp that he has left on art and which makes him unique among the artists of his time.

DORA VALLIER

MARC CHAGALL. Eliezer and Rebecca. Oil and gouache. 26½" x 20½". 1931.

The Russian years

by Manuel Gasser

Editor of «Du»

In his life and his creative activity, Marc Chagall's Russian years can be reckoned from his birth on 7 July 1887 to 1910, when he first went to live in Paris, then from 1914 to 1922, a good thirty years in all.

His first four years in Paris could also be considered "Russian" in some degree. Although this period had never been intended simply as an episode and although it was cut short by the outbreak of the first World War, Chagall was never more "Russian" than at the time of his first encounter and confrontation with the world of western Europe and its art. So considered, the "Russian years" take in the whole period of the artist's youth and development up to his thirty-fifth year, a portion of his life and of his artistic evolution in which he was not satisfied with laying down foundations for his work but in which he reached heights equal to the finest achievements of his future production.

The most important events of these thirty-five years are as follows:

Marc Chagall was born at Vitebsk in 1887 into a large family in modest circumstances. At that

The Chagall Family at Vitebsk. (Ida Meyer-Chagall Coll.).

time Vitebsk numbered about fifty thousand inhabitants, of whom half, including Chagall's parents, were Jewish. The boy attended the communal school till the age of nineteen when he was apprenticed to Jehuda Pen, a portraitist and genre-painter of the town. A year later, he became a pupil at the school in St. Petersburg financed by the "Imperial Society for the Encouragement of the Fine Arts". In 1908 he left this academy for a private art school and finally worked as a pupil of Leon Bakst. The most important event of the following year was to be his meeting with Bella Rosenfeld, his future wife.

At the end of the summer of 1910 he went to Paris, where he found his first studio in the Impasse du Maine. The following year he moved into *La Ruche* ("The Beehive"), the studio city in which Léger, Laurens, Modigliani and Archipenko were working at that time. However, his most fruitful contacts were not with painters, but with two writers, Blaise Cendrars and Guillaume Apollinaire. Through Apollinaire he also met Herwarth Walden, the champion of German expressionism.

In the spring of 1914 Walden organised Chagall's first one-man show in his Berlin gallery, *"Der Sturm"*. On this occasion the painter visited the German capital and decided to go on to Vitebsk.

A few weeks after his return to Russia the war broke out, and it was no longer possible to think of going back to Paris. Chagall had to limit his horizons once again to the narrow provincial life of the little town on the banks of the Dvina. In the following year he married Bella Rosenfeld, daughter of a rich Jewish dealer in jewellery, clocks and watches. Shortly after his marriage he was called up and posted to a service dealing with war economy in St. Petersburg, where his wife was able to join him with their little daughter Ida.

In St. Petersburg Chagall frequented intellectuals and artists who were to play their part after the October Revolution: Demian Bedny, the friend of Lenin, Alexander Block, Maïakowski and Pasternak among others.

For Chagall the 1917 Revolution meant the entry into possession of all civil rights which the Tzarist régime had denied to the Jews. But besides this it aroused hopes that the boldest dreams of the young generation of artists could now be realised.

On Bella's advice the painter abstained from taking an active part in cultural politics on the Governmental level and retired with his family to Vitebsk. There he pursued an intense and diverse activity in the cultural sector; he was appointed Commissar for the Arts in the old government of Vitebsk, and charged with the

MARC CHAGALL. Russian Peasants. 1912. 20⅛ x 15⅜ in.

organisation of art schools, museums, exhibitions, lectures and other manifestations.

He organised the celebrations of the first anniversary of the Revolution with a great display of flags, dioramas, triumphal arches etc.; in a former palace he set up a museum, a collective studio and an art school of which he was the director. But disillusionment was soon to follow this artistic springtime, so full of promise. Violent disputes broke out between Chagall's supporters and the "suprematists" led by Malevitch; Chagall offered his resignation, retired and definitely gave up his post of Commissar for the Arts in May.

Then he went to Moscow and for about a year devoted himself essentially to the theater.

Since before the Revolution he had designed decors for the producer Nicolas Evreïnov and later, for the Hermitage studio, he created sets for productions of the *Gamblers* and *Marriage* by Gogol, which, however, were never staged. This time all went very differently at the Jewish Arts Theatre of Moscow. Not only did he design the decors and the costumes, but also he decided on the style of the production and would not even delegate the task of making up the actors. And finally, and above all, he decorated the auditorium with a scheme of five mural paintings.

His last official activity in Soviet Russia concerned two colonies of war orphans; he taught drawing and painting to these abandoned children whom we saw come alive in the famous film *The Road to Life*. But relations with the bureaucrats concerned with culture grew more and more strained, and in the summer of 1922 Chagall, profiting from an invitation to exhibit his work in Berlin, left Russia with his family.

Now let us briefly consider the work he produced during these years.

In order to judge the originality of Chagall's first pictures and drawings it would be necessary to have a precise acquaintance with the work of his first masters and friends. His originality, however, appears strongly in the water color *The Musicians* of 1907. Though the fantastic element, which was to occupy such an important place in his future work, is not yet present in this popular scene, yet the Chagall we know is already contained in the way in which the figures and their village setting are conceived.

This manner and this state of mind or atmosphere are manifest even more clearly in the canvas *The Dead Man* of 1908. And in the following year, the portraitist in Chagall is revealed in a picture which many connoisseurs consider his best portrait, *My Fiancée in Black Gloves*.

The earliest pictures he painted in Paris seem at first sight to break the continuity of a line so powerfully affirmed. Chagall had to find his

MARC CHAGALL. The Artist's Sister. 1914. Private Coll., Leningrad.

Marc Chagall and his wife, Bella.

measure among the artistic currents of his new environment and he tried out the new means of expression he had thus acquired on the usual themes: landscapes of Paris, still life subjects, interiors, portraits and nudes. But very soon the Russian and Jewish inheritance reappeared forcefully and these new paintings are directly related to the Vitebsk work.

Although the first impulses Chagall received in Paris came from the Fauves, he soon fell under a cubist influence too, but we cannot properly speak of a "fauve" period any more than of a "cubist" period in the work of Chagall, and a canvas like *Homage to Apollinaire*, while doubtless remaining an important episode, is by no means essential in the general evolution of the artist.

The most important event of this first Paris period is certainly the series of masterpieces which are all dated 1911, even if, as Franz Meyer, Chagall's biographer, has shown, all these canvases can hardly have been painted in this single year. The mere enumeration of six of these pictures will be enough to show Chagall's astonishing creative power at this period: *To My Fiancée, To Russia, to the Donkeys and the Others, The Cabman Saint, I and the Village, Self Portrait With Seven fingers, The Poet.*

After this long series of great pictures from Paris there followed, on his return to his homeland, a group of works which were partly intimate, partly contemporary in character—a development which is easily explained by the simultaneous occurrence of private happiness and war experience.

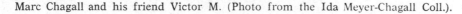

Marc Chagall and his friend Victor M. (Photo from the Ida Meyer-Chagall Coll.).

MARC CHAGALL. Composition. 1920-1922. 15 x 19½ in.

The state of mind of the happy husband and father is expressed in portraits, interiors and landscapes of deep lyrical content. The colors are delicate and exquisitely harmonious, the forms gentle and fluid; with a lover's care the painter has touched in the details of costume and setting of his models, so tenderly cherished by him. There is hardly a trace of the dramatic expression of his former scenes of popular and family life, of the demonism of a picture such as *To My Fiancée*. And when he clothes a beggar in the paternal prayer robe and phylacteries, he creates a masterpiece: *The Jew in Black and White,* so different from his old representations of the Jewish destiny, where power was charged with revolt. But in a later phase, in 1917 and 1918, the intimate and lyrical character of the portraits of Bella and the self portraits disappeared and in the paintings of couples, *Double Portrait With Glass of Wine* and *Above the Town,* the artist rediscovered the grand style of the masterpieces of 1911.

Running parallel to the portraits of the beloved woman and to other family pictures, there are works which testify to a very different inspiration.

Marc Chagall, Bella and little Ida. 1917.

MARC CHAGALL. War in the Palaces. Water Color. 1918. 13⅜ x 9 in. Tretiakoff Gallery, Moscow.

These are representations of soldiers, of wounded men and nurses, types and scenes which make us remember that Vitebsk was not very far from the front. They link up with those pictures of soldiers and policemen which played an important part in his early work and prove that the man in uniform, in the imagination of the painter, was of greater significance than simply as a picturesque figure.

In Chagall's work as a painter the five last Russian years occupy a fairly modest place, which is most understandable if we remember that he was in uniform for the first time and that later on, after the October Revolution, he was overwhelmed by cultural and administrative responsibilities.

On the other hand, Chagall's work for the theater during these years has assumed great importance. His sketches for decors and costumes are a turning-point in the history of the modern stage and his mural paintings made for the Jewish Arts Theater, the *Introduction to the Jewish Theater*, are numbered among his greatest masterpieces. In this decorative cycle which is the crowning achievement of the Russian years and one of the peaks of Chagall's whole work, we can see the rebirth in an astonishing and seductive manner of impulses absorbed from the cubists ten years earlier. In addition, these works, with all the related material, are not solely of interest to the historian of the art of the theater, they represent also a belated but nonetheless important chapter in the history of cubism.

MANUEL GASSER
Editor of "Du"

Marc Chagall teacher in an orphanage.

MARC CHAGALL. The Tribe of Dan. Detail. Stained-glass window in Jerusalem.

MARC CHAGALL. Model for the stained-glass window of « PEACE », (The Vision of Esau) for the United Nations Headquarters. 24¾ x 37¾ in. 1964. Me

the stained-glass window: 126⅝ x 190 in.

MARC CHAGALL.
The Creation of Man.
Metz Cathedral.

When Chagall hears the angels' singing

by Charles Marq

Technique is nothing other than the manner in which the artist uses his materials, and it is the finished work that shows his workmanship. There is no pre-established technique for work, and the first mosaics, the first frescoes, the first stained glass windows are no less perfect than those that came after. The painter does not make a separation between art and handicraft and all of our work with Marc Chagall is that mutual effort to invent at every instant, to never find oneself transposing.

Marc Chagall, similar perhaps in this respect to certain painters of the Renaissance at its apogee, has the gift of inspiring his collaborators. Far from asking them to adhere strictly to the model (a work perfect in itself and impossible to copy), he has a mysterious way of inciting others to relive his creation by means of another art. And the love that he demands has a force more powerful than the best intentions.

I remember our first conversations. Chagall had just been commissioned by Robert Renard to create the stained glass windows for the Metz cathedral. After the two small windows of Assy, this was quite another thing: a world of color and an immense space in the Gothic cathedral that he had to grasp and fill in. We spoke of the orientation of stained glass windows, of the way forms are reduced in a Gothic edifice, but above all, we talked of the light passing through the work, ready at any moment to make it explode with color, exalting the radiance of tones, transforming forms according to their transparency or their opacity, that sovereign power on which form and color depend. There was no question of technique, of lead, of the size of the glass... dead frameworks in which life itself would have wilted. Chagall was wrapped up in his vision, waiting for work to give it form.

A short time later, before the large models of the windows, I experienced the same feeling. How could I transmit that modulation, that luminous song of color? A thousand difficulties, even impossibilities, confronted me but I was conscious only of a deep desire to carry it out, of an ardor to give the painter's vision to the world.

In my studio I experimented with a scale of colors, seeking now in glass that suppleness, that continuity of light. Thus, I was gradually forced to make a complete scale of flashed glass that would permit a modulation within each piece of glass. By engraving with acid one obtains a shading off of value in the same tone right down to pure white, and this without the intermediary of the black lead setting. This light that is recaptured is, for me, the very life of the window for it is the white that makes colors live, determines them, defines them, limiting the optic blending and playing, in every case, the role of a passing tone as black does by means of grisaille.

After showing the model—the painter's first proposition—Chagall then awaited my own proposition, made this time in glass and lead. When he says, "Now show me what you know how to do"... it is actually an appeal to your freedom, to that faith in our poor hands, capable, God willing, of transmitting to creation. He shows with humility that his genius is greater than he, so great that it can also inhabit others.

How I admire his manner of being outside of himself when he arrives at the studio. My work is there, a window that concerns him in every way but for which he is not responsible. With what force he enters into that dispersed, stammering, skeletal reality! "I'll take everything," he says, not lingering over criticisms but knowing that he can make his own all those forms, those colors although they are still foreign to him. He harmonizes the pieces of glass, examining, correcting, touching on only a few essentials but with astonishing precision. And perhaps his love for France is so deeply rooted in that spirit of clairvoyance that it carries him into unreality.

Now the window is ready to be "done". The glassmaker, like Adam's clay, has fashioned the glass, the masses, the possible forms, the weight of color required, but the window is there like a lifeless being awaiting that first breath of life.

Chagall then begins to work before our dazzled eyes.

He enters the studio with the punctuality of an artisan who knows that work alone allows one to accomplish something, sometimes also with the precision of those tight-rope walkers whom he loves and who float up there in gravity by the grace of an immense daily labor.

An artisan finding life by the contact with materials, as poets or "poor men" by a contact

77

with flowers. A material which, he says, "is a talisman... to touch this talisman is a question of sentiment." Thought always says too much or too little and the intellect, for him, is left outside the door of the studio.

"In the soul there is a sort of intelligence, but in the intelligence there is not always a soul."

He paints. The grisaille, by the sole power of its value and of the line, permits him now to justify everything...

Form, that is his soul. In it there is neither an idea, nor a symbol, nor even reminiscence. I see a curve become, according to his inspiration, a plant, a flower, a face, an animal or a moon... or simply remain a curve.

An intensity of spirit that makes a new form spring forth. Infinite boundaries between order and disorder. He looks, moves away, rejects, begins again, going mysteriously towards a new image that he does not yet know.

The feeling he has about a subject dictates a line to him, a certain touch, and that touch enlightens him on his subject. The painting explains itself to the painter.

And in this ceaseless back and forth movement the window is born and gradually finds its form. There is no question of subject, technique, sentiment nor even sensitivity... only a mysterious relationship between light and eye, between grisaille and hand, between space and time... as if biological, as if molecular, becoming visible in rhythm, color and proportion. When the glass appears to have received its exact weight in grisaille, its proper quantity of life, the hand stops as if restrained by another hand. But any form that has not received all the painter's blood, dies, wilts, fades and disintegrates.

Chagall speaks of chemistry... No need to back away, this touch discloses the whole picture and this glass the whole window. Everything is there, everything is reassembled in every way in a living work. A touch born in a flash, produced by millions of years of accumulated forces or by a slow maturation of a gesture eternally repeated, an obscurely ripened deposit of effort. "Look at Rembrandt, look at Chardin, look at Monet—each has his own chemistry."

How, then, can one speak of technique when the "how to do" becomes the "how to be"? How can one speak of reason when I see the sublime fatigue of work destroy all determination to become only "color, light, liberty"?

Color... The impassioned weight of red, the infinite exchange of blue, the great repose of green, the dark mystery of violet, the implacable limit of yellow—here it is exalted in all the plenitude of its richness—and Chagall likes that color. But his color is something else.

"Ah! This isn't mere coloring. No question of red or blue there. Find your color and you've won the battle." The grisaille is spread in sheets, in accents, ordering, orchestrating by value until the moment when that sonority of color-sensation is perceived.

Light... "You kill it or it kills you and that's not it." Light that passes directly through the work to be painted, that animates it and gives it life; but light that must be tamed, directed, imprisoned in glass, allowed to live where it belongs.

"Stained glass is not easy. You must take it as one catches a mouse: not in a cage but with the hand. There are no 'in-betweens', it is yes or no."

Chagall scrapes, washes, repaints, becomes angry.

"What a nightmare! One must struggle with the lead: struggle, struggle, and then perhaps we'll win out."

"Ah! I don't know how to draw... One doesn't need to know how to draw. A line, that the good Lord knows how to do perfectly. When it's X or Y, it's still a line, it is not God. And so I make little dots, pricks, like that, full of little things of no importance."

His hand races over the glass, placing spots, lines, tints, stamps and marks for a whole hour...

"Ah! I have forgotten everything. Where am I?"

Liberty... the eternally repeated instant, a childhood that is his source and his goal. A childhood from which he emerged whole, from which he still draws his strength. As a painter he is like a newborn child. His anxieties, his torments, his long life of work have turned his hair white but for him painting begins at the break of day.

"The sign of a masterpiece is its freshness."

The inspired freshness of a Mozart, of a Schubert, whom he adores and who revive him after long hours of work.

A Schubert quartet... "That is what Art must be. Ah! Schubert, he cried because he had no friends, no love, nothing but look at what he has done to the whole world. Listen to the way he cries. I love that... Ah! How he suffered!"

He goes on working, becomes moved and thinks out loud. "One must caress. Nothing is given for free. Even the love of a dog must be won with a lump of sugar."

A quintet by Mozart... "Where did he unearth that? Someone whispered it to him... sing it... sing it, and he sings, he listens to what the angels tell him... that gift is not given to everyone... he does anything he wants, whether here or there, and it's right, always right."

Chagall continues his creation; his work accompanies him, and in the dazzling light of the creation I cannot distinguish one from the other.

This poet's dream of an ever new and luminous subject is perhaps what forces him to leave his completed work so quickly in order to go out and find the street and life—and to await the birth of a new dream tomorrow.

CHARLES MARQ

MARC CHAGALL. Model for the Rockefeller Chapel in New York. 1965.

MARC CHAGALL. Stained-glass window for Metz Cathedral. Detail. 1959-1960.

MARC CHAGALL. The Sacrifice of Abraham.
Stained-glass window
for Metz Cathedral. Detail.

MARC CHAGALL. The Dream of Jacob. Stained-glass window for Metz Cathedral. Detail.

The Jerusalem tapestries

by Maurice Cauchy

Head of the Gobelins Ateliers

Today three tapestries grace the walls of one of the largest halls in Jerusalem's Knesseth, three tapestries designed by Marc Chagall and executed in the high-warp ateliers of the Manufacture Nationale des Gobelins in Paris.

These three tapestries form a triptych 5 feet 8 inches high by 66 feet 4 inches wide; the surface area is over 1000 feet.

The triptych deals with three biblical themes that are part of the history of Israel. The work involves a combination of naturalism, supernaturalism and mysticism, and constantly attests

MARC CHAGALL. The Creation. Gobelins Works. 15 ft 8 in x 17 ft 11 in.

MARC CHAGALL. The Exodus. Gobelins Works. 15 ft 8 in x 30 ft.

to the artist's subtlety and imagination.

The panel on the right, "The Creation" (Marc Chagall called it "Peace") is a composition in which a mass of figures are arranged around the edge of a circle. In the center, men and animals are joined in peace. High in the middle, we have the fall of the Angel, Jacob's Dream; on the right, Moses and the Tables of the Law; on the left, the Crowd; on the lower left, the Mother and Child, on the right the Prophet. The presence of these latter figures may be an allusion to the New Testament (the cartoon is said to have been inspired by the Prophecies of Isaiah).

The panel in the middle, "The Exodus", is traversed, almost from end to end, by the Crowd, led by Moses and protected by the hovering Cloud. We see the Ark of the Covenant, the Adoration of the Golden Calf, Abraham's Sacrifice, Judith and Holophern. On the left are Rachel and King David, on the right Moses and the Tables of the Law; these frame the composition from top to bottom like cariatids. Standing out against the Cloud and the figure of King David is an angel holding the Torah and playing an ancient instrument; a view of the old city and the inscription in Hebrew characters "Jerusalem" lie between the Cloud and Moses; the burning village may be Sodom.

As for the "Entrance into Jerusalem," the Crowd from the biblical parts of the triptych seems to have invaded the panel on the right: led by King David, the people are carrying the Ark of the

84

Covenant, the Holy of Holies; they are accompanied by dancers and musicians. At the top center, Jerusalem is seen in all its radiant splendour (in printed Hebrew characters, we read: "Israel"); on the entire left-hand side of the composition, workers, builders and ploughsmen are busy at their tasks, while couples are dancing the Hora. The Israeli flag flies beside the figure of the first pioneer to return to the land of his ancestors (possibly in tribute to H. D. Gordon).

Clearly, this is a monumental work. It has been a long time since a work of this scope has come from the looms.

Marc Chagall's first cartoon was presented to the government agency in charge of Arts and Letters on November 30th, 1963 at exactly 3 PM.

MARC CHAGALL. The entry into Jerusalem. Gobelins Works. 15 ft 8 in x 17 ft 11 in.

It measured 4 feet 1 inch by 4 feet 10 inches. A photographic enlargement four times this size would be necessary to duplicate the actual dimensions of the tapestry. Now a blow-up of this size was very likely to distort the black and white values. It was therefore deemed more advisable to work from a color cartoon. For indeed, the material at hand has its own color laws. A method of color transposition seemed necessary (however, this approach was subsequently dropped). Once the problem was posed, Chagall's engraver, one Monsieur Sorlier was called in. It was decided to start with the figure of the Prophet in "The Creation", a fragment measuring 39 by 43 inches. The highwarp atelier was to weave this fragment and present it to the artist.

Once this procedure was agreed upon, the selection of the eighty colors that were to go into the design was begun. On March 11th, 1964, Madame Bourbonneux, assistant to the head of the atelier, who had been chosen for the test, began to weave her first "pick". On March 22nd, Marc Chagall made his first visit to the atelier

to supervise the interpretation and transposition tests, which went on until June 26th, 1964. The final result was presented to Marc Chagall and André Malraux, Minister of Culture, on July 1st.

On October 16th a second test was begun. This time the subject was a fragment of subtly shaded background involving the small figure of a musician. The work was to be done after a black and white cartoon. This test was completed on November 19th to Marc Chagall's entire satisfaction. This, then, would be the procedure adopted.

Orders were given to start the job.

On November 20th, 1964, the teams were formed.

On June 18th, 1969, the President of Israel, Zalman Chazar, the President of the Knesseth, Kadieh Lonz, Marc Chagall and his wife unveiled the three Gobelins tapestries before seven hundred guests, who were all thrilled by the great artist's first work in the field of tapestry.

MAURICE CAUCHY
Head of the Gobelins Ateliers

Chagall and the poets

by Jean - Jacques Lévêque

He is asleep / He is awake / Suddenly he paints / He takes a church and paints a church / He takes a cow and paints with a cow / With a sardine / With heads, hands, knives / He paints with a bull's sinew / He paints with all the dirty passions of a small Jewish town.

Most of us are acquainted with this poem by Blaise Cendrars, one of several that he dedicated to painting, to Chagall—for that lover of life,

of myths, and who had employed some rather ignominious epithets concerning art critics, was able in his poems of rare daring (especially at that time) to find the most striking counterpoints with plastic forms to accompany them. However, Chagall, undoubtedly because of the subjects he treats and because of his style, has found his best commentators among the poets. Furthermore, he created a large series of drawings, engravings

MARC CHAGALL.
Supposed portrait of Apollinaire.

and lithographs to illustrate many books such as Philippe Soupault ("Rose des Vents", 1920), Claire and Yvan Goll ("Poèmes d'Amour", 1925), Claire Goll ("Journal d'un Cheval", 1925), Jean Giraudoux, Paul Morand, Pierre Mac Orlan, André Salmon, Max Jacob, Jacques de Lacretelle, Joseph Kessel ("Les Sept Péchés Capitaux", 1926), Gustave Coquiot ("Suite Provinciale", 1927), Ilarie Voronca ("Ulysse dans la Cité", 1927), Marcel Arland ("Etapes", 1927), Paul Morand ("Ouvert la Nuit", 1927), Pierre Reverdy ("Pierres Blanches", 1930), Fernand Marc ("Poèmes", 1934), Yvan Goll ("Jean Sans Terre", 1936), Paul Eluard ("Le Dur Désir de Durer", 1946), Illiazd ("Poésies des Mots Inconnus", 1948); so many opportunities to bring to light the constant dialogue between a painter and poets. And we should not forget that Chagall himself is a poet as proved by the deluxe edition, published by Cramer in Geneva, of thirty of his poems, illustrated by twenty-four original wood engravings in color by the artist.

When Chagall arrived in Paris in 1910 it was during the effervescent period of Montparnasse. The painter first lived with his compatriot Ehrenbourg, Impasse du Maine, but he was attracted by "La Ruche", that high place of living art. La Ruche's title to glory is not only to have been the refuge of Léger and Soutine, but it was also where Cendrars, thanks to Chagall, discovered painting. It was also a time of friendship. Chagall made several sincere and valuable ones that accompanied his work in a time of complete evolution: Canudo, publisher of the review "Montjoie", Guillaume Apollinaire, of course, who was to write admirably about the painter, Léger, everyone's friend and also interested in poetry, Max Jacob who, like Chagall, inherited a rich folklore that was never dissociated from life, André Salmon, Roger de la Fresnaye, Robert Delaunay, Modigliani, André Lhote, Albert Gleizes, Maurice Raynal, Roger Allard, Dunoyer de Segonzac.

"The sky is blue. Dawn is breaking. Over there, farther away, cattle were being slaughtered, the cows were bellowing and I painted them": the same cows that Cendrars spoke of in his poems and that are also found in "I and the Village", in "Dedicated to my Fiancée", in "To Russia, to Donkeys and to Others", and in that prodigious "Self-Portrait with Seven Fingers". And space, so special for Chagall, in which objects, human beings and animals are no longer submitted to the law of gravity, gave Apollinaire the prophetic inspiration to call it "supernatural", a key-word that was to become for Pierre Albert-Birot "surrealist", later adopted by André Breton and his friends to make it famous.

For an exhibition in Berlin in "Der Sturm", after Klee and Kubin, Apollinaire wrote a preface that became, in the series "Calligrammes", the poem "Across Europe": "Rotsoge / Your scarlet face your biplane transformable into a hydroplane / Your round house where a red herring swims /

I must have the key to eyelids / Luckily we have seen M. Panado / And we are safe on that subject / What do you see my old M. D. / 90 or 324 a man in the air a calf that looks out from its mother's womb."

Thus, the first interlude ended, outside of Russia that he was later to refind at war and, soon after, in revolution. However, the letter from Blaise Cendrars, "Come back, you are famous and Vollard is waiting for you," was enough to bring him back to Paris to a studio where Lenin had lived, Avenue d'Orléans. In 1923, the surrealists rehabilitated the art of the unconscious mind, the virtues of madness, of desire, of the dream, of the irrational and a new quest for the Grail. Eluard, Ernst and Breton asked him to join them and, thus, Chagall became with others, and in spite of himself, and in virtue of a logic peculiar to surrealists, an artist worthy of appearing on the list of a movement which was taking an increasingly definite form and winning the interest of a larger public. However, the quality of this language that re-establishes the simple life, the magic of everyday living and distills a sort of wiseness, came to full bloom in the illustrations of the *Fables* of La Fontaine, commissioned by Ambroise Vollard in 1925. Soon after, he worked on "The Circus". Chagall's themes are always involved with the magical aspects of life. During this period he wrote *My Life*. Chagall walks straight into his legendary world; his relationship with poetry is suddenly blended with his relationship with life. Has he been done justice? André Breton in his penetrating studies on painting situates Chagall very precisely: "For a long time there existed a large gap in the origins of Dadaism and Surrealism—which were to bring about the fusion of poetry and the plastic arts—in that Chagall was not given enough credit. The poets themselves owe much to him—Apollinaire himself was inspired by Chagall in writing perhaps the "freest" poem of this century, "Across Europe", the Blaise Cendrars of "Trans-Siberian Prose"—right up to Maiakowsky and Essenine who speak of him in their most paroxysmal accents.

In writing an essay that remains among the most beautiful that has ever been written about him, Raisa Maritain spoke of Chagall as the "enchanted storm", thus establishing the close bonds that unite Chagall's earthly world with the forces of nature. "Humanity such as the painter sees it has neither turgidity nor grandiloquence: it is great only in his 'Prophets', it is brilliant only because of the painter's colors. His joy in love is grave. His gladness wrings one's heart with pity because it is so precarious, so vulnerable, having neither wealth nor strength to sustain it. These qualities make Chagall a primitive of the race of Christ and comparable to the great artists of the Middle Ages whose works also display that defenseless humility that calls for compassion and tenderness and characterizes the 'little ones' in whom God delights."

Here the poet gives the human measure of a work that does not cultivate the fantastic by refusing reality but, quite to the contrary, becomes a sort of elevation of that reality, a form of transcription on a sentimental level.

This fundamental understanding between the painter and the poets is centered in a well-defined domain that corresponds to the revelation of a marvelous realism in which painters, poets and even musicians cooperated at the beginning of the century. Each painter creates a geography according to certain unconscious impulses, the motors of the soul undoubtedly, and if one painter goes directly towards immediate reality, if another goes towards the cosmos, a last one will plunge into the crowd with the delight of a Peeping Tom. Chagall, true to himself, has decided to go towards the most natural and intemporal poetry. It is his element, his leaven. The blue and red rivers he makes flow through forests of heads, his animals endowed with wings that decuple space, his faces marked by the sign of recognition, his houses capsized like shipwrecks—in short, that universe both healthy but outmoded, supercharged by the power of dreams—are poetic space. The attraction this work has for poets is not the least proof that it can only be understood through poetry.

Aragon, curiously enough, recapturing the flame of the Cendrars of "La Ruche", writing recently "in the margin" or, more exactly, "in the wake" of Chagall's painting, in the perspective of those forms lifted up as if by "the miracle of the word", wrote: "You paint what you see like an apple on the table / And it will be the crossing of the Red Sea or the prediction / Of Angels at Abraham's where the tiling is the color / Of slaughter houses / For you tell the Bible better than anyone / And you do what the priest was told if the ulcer / Is caused by leprosy in vain did he wash it / Finding in fire only the hope to purify it / Painting evil so that it will disappear from earth / You paint torture and prophesied chastisements / You paint the war of the Kings and the tempest / The Plague with its black sails in the port / I could tell here the thousands and thousand of pictures that you will paint / If only the inspiration to kill goes as quickly as your brush."

A prophet, the poet in this case, like the painter, speaks of the multiple aspects of the world, of its instants, of its problems. It is a place of grief, of tears and joy of which, since the beginning of expression, art is made, whether by word or by image. Thus, Chagall has attained, not simply the secret of beings and things but the most total reality, the most general: the reality of legends.

JEAN-JACQUES LÉVÊQUE

MARC CHAGALL. The Poet Mazin. Oil.

Je n'entends pas un mot autour de moi
Des chemins, des forêts se croisent
J'aborde souriant ma journée
Et je t'attends encore. Pourquoi

Nuit et jour je porte une croix
On me pousse, on me traîne par la main
Déjà la nuit autour de moi
Tu t'éloignes, mon Dieu. Pourquoi

Poems by Marc Chagall, published in an edition *de grand luxe* by Cramer, Geneva, with 24 colored wood engravings is a collection of the most important poems written by the artist from 1930 to 1964. The only one of his earliest poems to appear in this volume is "Le Jardin" of 1909. The poems were translated by Philippe Jaccottet from a version by Professor Moshe Lazer, and with the collaboration of the painter. The poems "Si mon soleil" and "Seul est mien" were translated by Assia Lassaigne.

MARC CHAGALL. Engraving on wood for « Poèmes ». (Ed. Cramer).

MARC CHAGALL. Lithograph for Exodus. (Amiel, New York).

MARC CHAGALL. Self-portrait With a Goat. Lithograph. 1922-23. 16⅛ x 10⅜ in. Berlin.

Chagall as Engraver

by Robert Marteau

MARC CHAGALL. The Lovers Above the Town. Lithograph. 1921-23. Berlin. From the picture of 1917. 10¼ x 16 in.

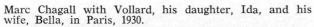

Marc Chagall with Vollard, his daughter, Ida, and his wife, Bella, in Paris, 1930.

Chagall arrived in Paris in 1910 and responded at once to the impact that it made on him. His personality was beginning to affirm itself even before the journey out of Russia: paintings such as *The Dead Man* or *The Burial*, painted in 1908 and 1909, are sufficient evidence of it. Now he was aware that above all he must preserve this nascent personality. He responded decisively, apparently foreseeing the whole direction in which the work that was to come must develop. "I had the impression that we were still just wandering around on the surface of matter, that we were still afraid of plunging into the chaos, of breaking up and trampling on the habitual surface of things... Down with naturalism, impressionism and realistic cubism... Welcome to the frenzy in us! A great bath of expiation. A fundamental revolution, not just a superficial one'.

He left Paris in 1914, and so parted from his friends Cendrars and Apollinaire, and went back to Vitebsk, the town where he was born. He was to come back to France only in 1923, after the war years and the revolution were over. He stopped in Berlin on the way, where he had left some canvases with Paul Cassirer, the art publisher. The stay in Germany had a decisive influence, for it was there that he began to learn engraving in all its techniques, in Struck's atelier:

drypoint, eau-forte, wood engraving and litho-graphy. Franz Meyer states in his book *Marc Chagall, l'œuvre gravé:* "He owed his interest in graphic expression to the initial stimulus that Cassirer and Feilchenfeldt gave him. But even more", he adds, "to his stay in Germany, the classic home of engraving, where the Expres-sionists had quite recently engraved their most powerful works, using the techniques of wood engraving and eau-forte".

Chagall had the manuscript of *Ma Vie* with him, which had been written in Russia, and he began to illustrate it for Cassirer. Translation difficulties prevented the text from being published in German. But he finished the plates, some of which took up themes that he had already used in his paintings. The majority welled up from the intensely vivid memories collected in *Ma Vie:* plate 2, for example, which tells the episode of his grandfather retreating to the roof of the house for a bit of peace and quiet while he ate some carrots. This comic story reveals Chagall's predilection for the precise little events, extra-ordinary but entirely anodine, which imperceptibly dislocate the serious, customary, orderly world. We see him conniving with the unexpected, observing what happens with a child's perpetual surprise at the world about him. We also see how, working in what for him was still a new technique, he at once used it to acquire a greater freedom: he put aside the rigor of the metal plate for more spontaneity, for what was *painted from life.* Everything is hanging, in suspense, askew, expectant, searching, shaky, in process of appearing, of flowering. What is as it is now was not like this a second ago, and will be something else again in an instant.

The predilection for ascension that we notice in this anecdote was to be a constant in Chagall's temperament. It was affirmed with *The pro-menade,* where the fiancée glides sky-high over the roofs of the town, held by her fiancé's hand. His prismatic suit is in memory of cubism. A symbol of ascension that is present in many other paintings is the ladder, which we find again in *The Lovers at the Fence.* In *The House in Vitebsk* a whole team in harness has taken to the air, so that the landscape may assume the reality proper to memory. Memory merely seizes on some point that the senses have registered, in order to come flying towards us borne up on emotion. Chagall constantly invents the signs for this, and so charges the world with an illuminating poetic intensity: what is external can only really be seen as it truly is by inner vibrations. In this way, when Chagall engraves *At the Easel,* he doesn't hesitate about transcribing the subjective truth of the upheaval worked in someone who looks closely at the world and is *transported* by what he sees—or by passion. Such a man is uprooted from the earth, he walks on air. We see the same thing in his *The Lovers by the River*

MARC CHAGALL. Engraving. (Cassirer, Berlin, 1923).

MARC CHAGALL. Engraving for the Bible (Ed. Verve)

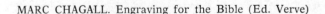

or again in *Above the City*, a black and white lithograph of 1922-23. This was one of the first he made, together with *The Man with Sideburns*.

When Chagall came back to Paris in 1923 he got to know Vollard, and undertook the illustration of Gogol's *Dead Souls* for him. Whereas in *My Life* drypoint was the dominating process, Chagall was now to use eau-forte as his major graphic technique.

Did Chagall himself suggest *Dead Souls* to Vollard? It wouldn't surprise us, especially when we remember that Dostoievski declared that every Russian was in debt to Gogol, just as one might say of every Spaniard that he owes something to Cervantes. In any case Chagall was to go on making pictures of the Russia of his childhood and adolescence, for the most part. The acuity of his vision strikes us immediately: there is nothing bookish about it. Life is seized in the very process, in all its daily aspects. Fantasy was to be the very essence of his art. In *Arrival of Tchitchikov, The Traktir, The Town* Chagall is still close to the style of *My Life*, only more richly voluble, so to speak. He is freer in expression, in verve, even in the composition itself, which gives the effect of being utterly unpremeditated. Objects and people are placed with a casualness that excludes any deliberate setting of the scene.

Two ways, it seems to us, soon began to attract him: *the pictorial way* and *the linear way*, we could call them. The former seeks what is melting or blended, the nuance, the passage of light and color through the gradation of blacks. The latter works towards elegance of line, in its suppleness, its refinement, and its concern to give life to the white. So far from being diverging, these two ways are mutually supporting, either by contrast and opposition, or by uniting so totally together that we are held really fascinated. *The Old Park of Pliouchkine* is a case in point. The whole block abounds in detail, without its being in the least worked over and made heavy in execution. For it never ceases to take wing, to be exuberant, a filigree, with a shifting sky stirred up above the horizontal, ruinous, heavy hut that is itself pulled right towards the bottom of the picture. Elsewhere, tenderly humorous, and with a light, refined line, he depicts the young country girl with her big feet and rough outward appearance, showing the way to a hairy and bearded coachman. He also exaggerates Madame Korobotchka, "one of those good women forever declaring—head on one side—how poor they are, but who nevertheless gradually fill up the canvas bags hidden away in their cupboard drawers". The contrast between the old shrew's bloated face and huge, grasping hands (one of which has been still further thickened with aquatint) and the drawn ornament that gives a light touch to her dress and the quilt is remarkable. And all is grace and sensitive whorls in the architecture and landscape of *The traktir's House*. It adds to the comedy of the characters,

those solemn puppets in a theater which they remain oblivious. The pictorial way is doubtless at its peak in *Tchitchikov on His Bed*. It could all be in color, so vibrant are the black lines— now free, now coagulated together, and at times distorted as though by childish laughter welling up at the sight of Tchitchikov straining to hoist his great naked buttocks up onto the bed.

An entire human comedy unfolds before our eyes. In *The Painters* the painters are painting a room white and the people and objects in it are having a high old time. This clearly terrifies the owner who, as host, is about to do the honors for his guests. In *The Witnesses*, each one, gesticulating, and given life by the fine, open line, is seized in movement and the heat of action; in *The Fleeing Naked Man* the tax assessor Drobjachkine, threatened by the peasants brandishing their implements, goes back to the fields and the cows and along with his clothes abandons house, bed, and the wife who lies in it; or in *The Toothache*, where the violence of the line makes us realize the rage and pain that the hero Tchitchikov is suffering.

I would like to note that Chagall always avoids caricature and satire. He prefers a tender, earthy poetry, full of vitality. Observation is what feeds this verve, always. Nothing is set, nothing fixed: people and objects take life under the graver without our expecting it to happen, and their *geste* follows its course under our gaze amid the tribulations, joys and jokes that each new day brings. We always feel how greatly life delights him, but Chagall adds a dimension to the fleeting manifestations of life that he seizes, and this extra dimension puts the work far above any mere realism limited to particular situations.

In 1927 he undertook to illustrate the *Fables of La Fontaine*, again for Vollard. He was turning over *The Circus* in his mind at this same period, and there exist a few plates for it dating from this time. But the work was to be carried out in lithography after the Second World War, and it was published by Tériade in 1967. *The woman Circus Rider* dates from 1929: she is graved as if with the point of a thorn on springtime's skin, and she barely touches the back of the fabulous dream-horse. You could believe that her slender body will be bent at any moment by a breath of wind. Her hair and the horse's mane have the same wavy ringlets. Her arms are over her head in the form of the handle of a basket, as willowy as what they imitate. But Chagall was working on the *Fables* in a completely different spirit, as he elaborated the bestiary with its inextricable mixture of humanity. The point I am making is most readily understood by reference to Franz Meyer's text *(Marc Chagall, l'œuvre gravé)*, introducing the way Chagall approaches La Fontaine's world: "To begin with, Chagall thought in terms of color plates, worked on copper from his gouaches. But it turned out to be too difficult a

piece of craftsmanship to transpose the originals, because of their rich coloring. So he had to give up the idea of color, and he became a black and white engraver again to make the set. Yet the color that was in the gouaches is all there in the black and white of the eau-forte. The result comes from bringing several techniques together: first he engraves, then he covers the engraved parts with a touching-up varnish and so gets very marked painting effects. The needle draws leaves and thickets in their finest ramifications, conveys the complexity of feathering or of supple fur, and manages by lines and hatching to give the richest gradation from white to black, obtained by profuse scoring and counter-scoring. In some instances Chagall also uses a brush with multiple points, and in this way is able to modulate the values up to intense black. On top of it all the brush introduces light, in flashes, in areas, in lacework, brilliantly white against the blacks and the gamut of grays. In some places the whites then have eau-forte lines engraved in them. Each plate is thus the result of many cumulative phases, during which the structure of dark and light is slowly elaborated. The process is comparable to the stages in which the color construction of a painting is worked out".

Often Chagall likes to stress what is mythical and universal in a fable, as in *The Lion in Love*, for example, which he links with *Beauty and the Beast*. Tragedy and terror heighten the theme, and it is intensified by the tight network of fine lacerations which sometimes hems the protagonists in and sometimes coagulates in patches or in thick rings. In *The Old Woman and the Two Servants* he exalts the young unclad bodies, crushed with exhaustion, by a lunar whiteness, and their brilliance forces the old shrew back into the shadows. He has made the splendid cock all swollen with vanity, lost in admiration before the pearl of his own silliness.

Chagall takes one detail or another that has moved him and uses it as a base, and so his own poem interweaves with La Fontaine's and a whole world emerges, at the extreme limit of the division between animal and human. Each character appears on the stage in all his complexity: for example, that other cock *(The Rooster and the Fox)* perched up in the tree, his mistrust plain to see in every line, down to the very set of his legs. As for the lion in *The Lion Grown Old*, he has assumed a human face: an infinite sadness possesses him, yet we get no impression of bitterness, nor of resignation, only something enigmatic that relates him to the sphinx.

In 1931 Chagall went off to Egypt, Syria and Palestine. On his return he devoted himself almost entirely to the illustration of *The Bible*. He worked on it up to 1939. That was the year of his journey to Holland, on the eve of the catastrophe: in that light it takes on the aspect of a real pilgrimage to Rembrandt. He was far away from France until 1948 and took up his work on the Bible again only in 1952.

The Bible is unquestionably Chagall's masterpiece so far as engraving on copper is concerned, and no doubt it is the single greatest masterpiece of engraving of our age. It becomes plain that everything previous to the Bible found its fulfillment in the Old Testament pictures. The anecdotes and observation of *My Life*, the spontaneity and perspicacity of *Dead Souls*, the understanding and technical knowledge of *The Fables of La Fontaine*: these all come together in *The Bible*, and the flowering is complete. Looking at these 105 eau-fortes, you would think Chagall learned how to engrave in Berlin with the one intention of going back to the source of the Hebrew soul; you would think he had been building up his strength for years in order to respond to the Word of his people and bring his contribution to the Book. Elsewhere he could show only facets of his spirit; here spirituality itself unfolds, the mighty breath of the poet-prophets. Fable takes on its real dimension, in the origin and creation of the world; to speak is to create; the word is lightning; the poem is made of stars, nights, days, dawn, water, woman; the man-shepherd receives the divine Word, comes down from the mountain, and transmits it. The living God reveals himself, the dove is the winged symbol from whom salvation is looked for; the angels, stilling their white wings, grow visible to Abraham's eyes, and the earth is present all around them just as they themselves are truly present without old Melchisadek the priest showing any sign of surprise; yes, they have taken on the reality which is now there in the hand that Abraham raises in front of his face, in *Abraham Mourning Sarah*. Then there is Joseph, full of music and sun like the shepherd Apollo, in the middle of his flock, a premonitory figure of the one who, like himself, is to be sold. The prophets are afraid at their vision, or afraid at the Word which they alone hear; God is the only witness of their solitude and suffering; the heavens open, Jerusalem perishes, and the living are clearly one with the dead, left standing upright only to weep. Chagall makes the great drama and the tribulation his own; and the tempest that shakes him is transmitted to the paper in its violence, its gravity, its amplitude: what is happening here and now, around this well, amid this flock, is at the epicenter of the great theater of the world.

We can really understand, then, that he truly did go to Holland as a pilgrim, to Rembrandt; he went to pay homage to the man who, like himself, had the gift of making the divine acts find access to the visible world. Complete mastery of technique leads the hand in this work to respond to every vibration of the soul. All is softly bound together. The eye searches the surface as though with hands, is enthralled, and cannot tear itself away.

MARC CHAGALL. Litograph in color for "Daphnis and Chloe". (Ed. Verve. 1964).

From this moment on, as though he had the intimate conviction of having reached a summit in this art and in this technique, and that no wave could lift him higher and no river carry him further on, as the work began to be finished Chagall turned more than ever to color, and required of lithography that it should answer to another side of his painting. He had made 13 lithographs in New York for *Four Tales of a Thousand and One Nights*. He renewed the link with Paris again by making nine other lithographs published in 1954 in the review *Derrière le miroir* under the title *Paris*. In the same year he made his second visit to Greece and painted several gouaches. The plates for *Daphnis and Chloe* were to come out of these gouaches. The choice of the Greek text, full of fresh, sensual poetry, and his first visit to Greece, date from 1952.

Chagall always found it essential to walk over the ground of whatever country he had chosen for a work, and to see, feel, test the light and colours, and get to know the people. He did not undertake *The Bible* without visiting the land of his people, and he did not allow himself to decide on the colors for *Daphnis and Chloe* without first having had physical contact with the light and the sea and the land of Greece. True poet that he is, Chagall always works from what is concrete. That is where he found the life-giving joy that breaks through naturalistic appearances, causes forms to burst open like undreamed-of flowers, splashes color on the sky and the fields and in the fathomless depths of the sea, so that the soft sounds of grasses, rivers, trees and lambs commingle with the lovers.

MARC CHAGALL. Litograph in color for "Daphnis and Chloe".

A set of lithographs was published by Tériade in 1967 with the title *The Circus*. Chagall wrote the accompanying text-poem. In a sense it was an extension of *My Life*, which in 1922 was itself the point of departure for his engraved work.

This reminder comes quite naturally, for *The Circus* is not a work simply illustrating the circus in words and pictures. Perhaps above all else it is a secret testament, in which Chagall gives free play to the telling of his secrets. Again, it is a journal, or a fresco in which the human comedy is made to unfold and is denounced for what it is, or a miror in whose greatly reduced space is reflected everything that becomes exhausted or dissolved in day-to-day living. It is a way of saying that for Chagall the circle of the circus ring is magical only in so far as it encloses what is essential: each gesture and attitude being raised to the level of sign and symbol. For nothing is natural here, though all seems to be, thanks to an art and artifice based on the precise observation of instincts, habits and behavior. Is not the circus, by its very form, a replica of the universe, a world in which the impossible is still about to be annihilated at any moment? The girl on the trapeze goes from star to star; the horse and its rider make poetry spring from its source; men and animals begin to converse with each other again... Childhood marvels at a daylight that is almost the pristine light.

No, it is not a dream; only a reality slightly beyond the exchanges of every day. Chagall knows in a flash how to disclose this reality to us, by a surreptitious displacing of objects and people and a substituting of the true color for the expected color. In this way he creates relationships of enchantment, surprise and play, where what is grave banishes what is merely serious; passages and crossing places where comedy, drama, grace and humor are suddenly swallowed up; planets where what is imaginary is part of reality, not an effort to escape.

"It seems to me", says Chagall, "that I would have lacked something if, aside from color, I had not also busied myself at a moment of my life with engravings and lithographs.

From my earliest youth, when I first began to use a pencil, I searched for that something that could spread out like a great river pouring from the distant, beckoning shores.

When I held a lithographic stone or a copper plate, it seemed to me that I was touching a talisman. It seemed to me that I could put all my sorrows and my joys into them... everything that has crossed my life in the course of the years: births, deaths, marriages, flowers, animals, birds, poor working people, parents, lovers in the night, Biblical prophets, in the street, in the home, in the Temple and in the sky. And as I grew old, the tragedy of life within us and around us."

ROBERT MARTEAU

MARC CHAGALL. Blue Landscape. Original lithograph in color. (Ed. Maeght).

100

Chagall and the theater

by Denis Milhau

Curator of the Musée des Augustins

The impressive list of ballets for which Chagall did the decor is sufficiently well known for us to be able to form some idea of the role he has played in the history of the modern theater. But this participation in the world of choreography, based as it is on the requirements of an empty stage and the narrative and descriptive needs of backdrops illustrating what the ballet develops in a non-naturalistic way (whatever the choreographer's aesthetics may be), is basically the least theatrical element in Chagall's work. The imagery is dictated by the obligatory front view of the ballet stage, which every commission that was suggested to him entailed, and involved a mere extension of that imagery to the required monumental dimensions. Similarly the art of fantastic and poetic story-telling that he brought to the decor is merely a variant of his easel painting.

Two groups of Chagall's works do point, however, to a dramatic and theatrical preoccupation of a special order: the adaptation of Chagall's original, proper imagery to the invention of new space relationships—arbitrary, but nonetheless real and specific—in order to create a new dramatic milieu. For the ballet, by contrast, Chagall had merely to cope with a transposition of the dimensions of his paintings. These two groups of works are, firstly, the commissions he carried out from 1915 to 1922 for the regular

MARC CHAGALL. Design for the curtain of the Jewish Theater in Moscow. 1918.

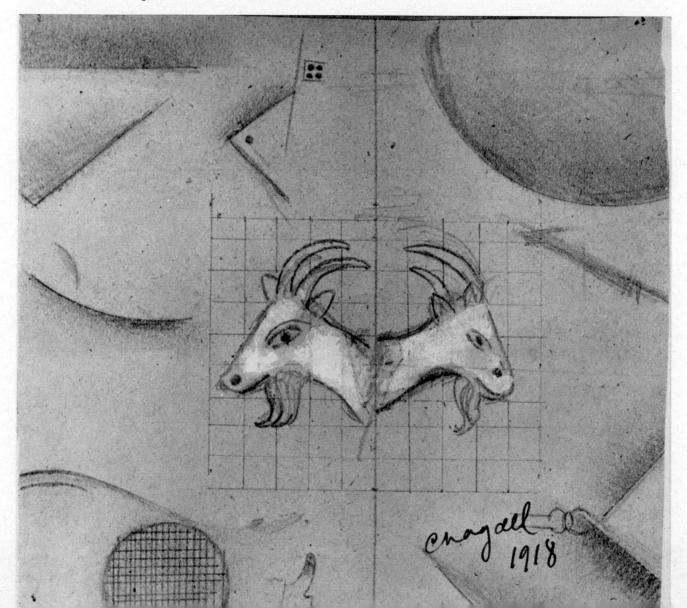

Marc Chagall painting sketches for the Jewish Theater.

theater and, secondly, his various monumental decorations for theaters and auditoriums.

Up to the beginning of our century, any painter called upon to work for the theater was invited to mount a decor which, whatever its plastic qualities might be (thanks to this or that man's powers of pictorial invention), remained a decor in the strict meaning of the word: i.e. a picture *in front of* which a story was to be enacted. So the theater called in painters to work for it in just the way that Chagall worked for the ballet. Apart from the choreographic forms that have come into being since the war and have taken the lead in dramatic spatial research, without Chagall's being called upon to make any contribution, the world of ballet remained a world of beautiful fairy tales. Chagall, therefore, whose world was closest to the fairy-tale world, must be required to give it its decors.

But when he really did get to grips with the theater Chagall discovered the real problems of theatrical space, and brought an original solution to them. Was it intention or luck, chance or premeditation? Chagall's contact with the theater was made through a small group of men who were much attacked and vituperated. They had set out to destroy the pictorial conception and the impossible naturalism of a theater that remained a willing prisoner of the Italian model. Its last representatives were Stanislawsky and later on even Brecht. The group was Meyerhold's "Théâtre de Style", and Chagall met them thanks to the playwright Nicolas Evreinoff. Meyerhold did not envisage the theater as a shut-in place confronting the equally shut-in space where the audience sat, nor as a place in which a representation of the real world should unfold. For him the theater was something wholly fabricated, a work of art, from the spoken text to the actors' interpretation of it. It certainly must not try to deceive, must not attempt to create the illusion of being reality in the guise of a play. It must be a total work of art, fulfilling its poetic, didactic, and mythical function in the form of a show, by creating the necessary conditions for the spectators' real participation: a work of art present by the fact of being presented, not a mere illusion of some false reality.

The creators of the "Théâtre de Style" were opposed to naturalism in all its manifestations. They were in complete sympathy with every art form—whether painting, literature, or music—which successfully affirmed the prerogatives of invention and transposition and the specificity of its own productions. Chagall had returned to France with his highly original plastic style, which had developed from his assimilation of fauvism and cubism to his own figurative predilection, with all its fantastic, surrealistic and poetic realism. He became a privileged partner of the group. As Apollinaire first suspected and then proclaimed aloud, he was both painter and poet,

Marc Chagall and Michoels, the actor, in Moscow.

poet and painter, the one conditioning the other.
Other painters, by contrast, were either illustra-
tors only, in the illusionistic sense of the word,
or else they were deliberately opposed to any
objective signification, any figurative representation whatsoever of anything at all that could be
seen or said. Chagall's very nature drew him to
the "Théâtre de Style", just because of his being
both painter and poet. The meeting was charac-
terized by such identity of views that from the
very first works done in common, in 1915, Chagall
could quite happily take up again some of the
paintings he had already done, and use them for
sets and sketches. Thus for Evreinoff's *To Die
Happy* he simply took up *The Drinker* of 1912
again: his works had enough "style" to adapt
themselves to what Meyerhold's group expected.
It might seem that you could accuse Chagall of
still being just an easel painter blowing his works
up to much larger dimensions, the only difference
from other established decor painters lying in the
stylization. But Chagall's works between 1910
and 1920 present such a tremendous modification
in painting of the way of representing space that
their transfer to the theater entailed in itself a
modification of the nature of decor as it was
traditionally understood. With sets such as these
the producer was not given a picture *in front of*
which he would dispose the action. He was
compelled to give the action back its rightful
space, i.e. the whole of the stage area.

Between 1917 and 1921 Chagall suggested sets
and designs for curtains and costumes either for
Meyerhold or for the "Ermitage experimental
theater" or for the "Moscow revolutionary satirical
theater" or even in the end for Stanislawsky, the
plays being by Gogol ("The Government Inspec-
tor", "The Gamblers", "Marriage") or by Synge
("The Playboy of the Western World"). But none
of them was carried out. The new aesthetic being
proposed was too premature, and came up against
every imaginable difficulty. All Chagall got from
the authorities was a long series of refusals.

In these sets, especially the ones for Synge,
what we have is by no means a description of an
enclosed scene on the stage, in the form of a
beautiful picture which the producer has only to
spread out and so fix decorative walls for his
acting space. What we find instead, in addition
to expressive stylized research for characters and
costumes, are images for the sets that are a
synthesis of the front and perspective views of
the stage and of the aerial view of the same
stage area, in plan. This means that the entire
space, in all its dimensions, becomes the dramatic
setting for the action, and not a framework for
the decor. The walls disappear, leaving the stage
area open on all four sides. So the designs

provoked one of the first known breaks with the sacrosanct traditional opposition or confrontation of the spectators' social area and the dramatic area. Chagall is, thus, one of the people who invented the replacing by scenic elements of the framework decor in the form of a descriptive picture of a fully determined place. In the old tradition the theater was thought of as being a "tableau vivant", and the painter indicated a realistic decor, in perspective, on a flat-surface picture. That tradition gives place, with Chagall, to plastic animation of the dramatic area as a whole.

Chagall's only works in this field that were actually carried out, in the period 1919-1921, were the decors and costumes for some little plays, some "miniatures" by Sholem Aleikhem for the "Moscow theater of Jewish art" directed by Efross and Granowsky. They were in the same style and spirit as the Gogol and Synge projects. There the first group of works by Chagall, in which he solved the problem of a theater that was conscious of its true nature, unfortunately comes to an end. Thereafter people took care to demand of Chagall that he remain simply a prodigious illustrator. I mean by this that his illustrations truly are prodigious, but that he was never again authorized to live and act what we could call the real adventure of the theater. The adventure itself was forbidden in the theatrical world, or else it was condemned to that clandestine struggle which is the lot of revolutionaries, in the cultural domain as well as in others.

The second group of works, doubtless more illustrative in character than the first, is interesting for a different reason. It is the group of decorations for theaters and theater halls that stand out as landmarks in Chagall's career: 1921, decoration of the "Moscow Jewish art theater"; 1949, decoration of the foyer of the "Winter Gate Theater" in London; 1959, the foyer of Frankfort theater; 1963, the ceiling of the Paris Opera; 1966, the Foyer of the "Lincoln Art Center" in New York.

The foyer decorations presented no specific problems, but the hall decorations belong to a certain conception of the theater as a place of communal celebration. At the "Moscow Jewish art theater", which occupied a small rectangular hall that had not been designed for this use, the decoration consisted of a long fresco on one of the longer walls and facing it four compositions on wall sections between windows, together with a stage curtain. The four compositions are allegorical figures of Music, Dance, Literature, and Theater; they are large, cubist figures, dynamic and full of color, at the same time Biblical and bannal in character. The same is true of the stage curtain, representing love in the theater. The fresco is an introduction to Jewish theater, a sort of satirical and picaresque procession of theater and circus characters and accessories. It

takes the path of a long ascending diagonal, applied over an abstract, geometrical, ground of bands and circles that accentuate the discursive movement. The style inherent in these monumental decorations, which transform the social area of the ground floor into a space of the same nature as the dramatic space confronting it, is the same as that used for the scene on-stage in the plays put on at the theater with Chagall's decors. Thus the ornamentation of the auditorium was no longer a mere prettifying of the walls: in effect it was all part of the invention of that particular, artificial place which the theater in its entirety is.

At the Paris Opera the ceiling is part and parcel of the extraordinary decor which the architecture of the Palais Garnier itself constitutes. Chagall found that he was obliged to respect the amphitheater as being a separate entity, intentionally sharply divided from the stage area, so as to face it. He accepted the challenge, and worked in such a way as imperceptibly to reunite all the separate elements. He created a ceiling that was sumptuous and at the same time discreet. It is based on the circle and the cross, and makes systematic play with asymmetry and displaced motifs. The garland motif appears to be divided up in obedience to the cross, but in fact it obeys the pentagon; although it is apparently balanced by the cardinal diameters and punctuated by a clearly separated central motif, the garland of the motif in concentric registers never actually converges toward the middle nor is it ever divided equally by the diameters. The effect is one of equilibrium and regularity, whereas really the composition is a mass of small but appreciable displaced elements and of dynamically swirling and off-balance units, on the bias. The sky wells up, all movement and scintillation, leading the eye towards the stage area; yet at the same time it holds to its proper place, and is in keeping with the opulent and showy diapason of Garnier's style, by its proper fantasy and baroque spirit.

I must be excused for adding a word to the quarrel that arose from the commissioning of this ceiling; the ceiling is well and truly there, in place, and you have to have looked at it in the course of a performance to understand how great a work of art it is and see how, at the age of 76, Chagall did victorious battle with the space, the theater and the architecture—with what wonderful spirit and fervor—and by his talent put life into them. In the Metz windows and the Jerusalem windows the visionary maker of images had already proved that he knew how it could be done.

DENIS MILHAU
Curator of the Musée des Augustins, Toulouse.

MARC CHAGALL. Costume for the Ballet *Aleko*.

MARC CHAGALL. *The Firebird*. Opening Curtain.

MARC CHAGALL. Costume for the Ballet *The Firebird*.

In Alice's wonderland

by Gilbert Lascault

MARC CHAGALL. Lithograph for the Circus (Tériade, Paris).

CHAGALL AND HEADS

One must first *describe* the prodigies that populate Chagall's world and, in a way, constitute the symbol, the descriptive stamp. That which in other universes (that of bannal perception, for example), seems exceptional, the monstrous, the disquieting becomes an everyday reality here: we experience, at the level of the visible, the omnipotence of God's desires. These desires have a *style* for which we need an attentive description of forms in order to understand them.

It is just as frequent, just as normal to have two faces as it is to have one. For example, in "The Soul of the City" (1946), the painter has two faces, as in "Paris Seen from the Window" (1913), the man we see near a cat with a human head; like the nude woman in "The Tree of Jesse" (1960); like the famous "Bride" of 1927. Try as one may, one nonetheless thinks of Georges Bataille, even though his tragic universe seems to be diametrically opposed to that of Chagall's: "Finally I have more than one face. And I know which one is laughing at the other."

It also happens that the face turns upside down: the eyes are just above the neck, surmounted by the nose and mouth. The inverted faces of "The Poet" (1911-1912), of the sketch of the curtain for "The Firebird" (1945), of "The Yellow Room" (1910). It was perhaps the memory of his father's reflection in the water that imposed this form on Chagall: "Deep in the water, his head upside down, scarcely moving, was the reflection of my father. He, too, shakes from his clothing the dust of minor sins," as he wrote in *My Life*.

The transformation of the human body is sometimes discreet. Without the title, only an attentive spectator would notice the seven fingers in "The Self-Portrait with Seven Fingers" (1911-1912). Just as the wolf in *Little Red Riding Hood* has big teeth the better to eat you up, so the painter multiplies his fingers the better to paint the universe he founded.

Members become isolated; they leave the body which limits their autonomy. In "The Circus" (1956), one person seems to be juggling with his own head. "The Drunkard" (1911-1912), is a body whose head has detached itself to go join the bottle. Desire is stronger than anatomy. One must wish to be headless. A milkmaid flies, leaving her head behind, ("To Russia, to Donkeys and to Others", 1911). This is to have your mind elsewhere: Chagall, just as in a dream, takes expressions literally. As a child he felt his head leave his body and he describes this in *My Life:* "I like to cry a little when the 'badchan', in a high voice, sings and yells, 'Fiancée, fiancée, think a little about what awaits you!' What awaits you? On hearing these words, my head gently detaches itself from my body and cries somewhere near the kitchens where fish are being prepared."

THE RULES OF MIRAGES

Human elements and animal elements blend together to make up a monstrous body that Chagall's art shows in a marvelous harmony. Contrary to the works of Bosch, Breughel or Odilon Redon, Chagall offers us the gracefulness of monsters. It is pleasant for a bride to have the tail of a fish instead of legs ("The Mermaid's Tail", 1945). In "The Descent from the Cross" (1947), the person who piously takes Christ down has a bird's head. A winged fish plays a violin; to hold the instrument, a hand emerges from its mouth, ("Time has no Shores", 1930-39). The "Dance" (1930) presents a sort of minotaur; another minotaur accompanies with a violin "The Violoncellist" (1939), whose body has changed into an instrument; a third embraces a bride. ("Midsummer Night's Dream", 1939). A bird adopts a feminine face ("The Village of Dark Sun", 1950; "The Flutist", 1954). A four-legged animal occupies the sky; his human face topped by a felt hat ("While Listening to the Rooster", 1944).

Objects, too, enter into strange combinations that permit them to live. With two feet a lamp post can walk ("Dusk", 1943). In an engraving made in America during the war, an Eiffel Tower has one eye and hair and it places a giant hand in front of its "face". In the "Newlyweds of the Eiffel Tower" (1938-1939), a violin becomes the body of a cow.

Chagall's world is a separate, different universe, a place of refuge, of liberty. It is understandable that he sometimes dreams of giving shelter to the persecuted: "I would like to transport them to my canvases to keep them safe."

In this strange world, physical laws no longer count. Cows, women, old men and lovers float in his sky: there is no law of gravity. In a much more violent way, Goya in his "Caprices" drew in his sky a *rain of bulls* (Lluvia de Toros). Several times in *My Life*, Chagall speaks of his daydreams about flying, of elevation, always with a marvelous prosaism: "It seemed to me that I was rising to the sky, through the birches, the snow, the clouds of smoke, with their plump women and those bearded peasants who tirelessly crossed themselves." Opaque bodies become transparent: the colt is seen in the mare's belly as she pulls the cart of "The Cattle Merchant" (1912), like the child standing up in his mother's womb ("The Pregnant Woman", 1913). Secrets are brought to light: those of life.

As in *Alice in Wonderland*, in Chagall's paintings, size is never standard: on a gigantic cow's head a tiny milkmaid milks a miniature cow ("I and the Village", 1911) while houses stand on their bases or on the tip of their roofs. When "The Soldier Drinks" (1912-13), he see himself as a tiny man on the table where he has placed his glass, caressing a tiny woman. In this unusual cosmos the upper and lower cease to have any precise direction; everything is *topsy-turvy:* everything is desoriented, confused, finds its bases collapsing beneath it; paradoxically, sense no longer makes sense. A tree is born from the sky ("While Listening to the Rooster", 1944); others grow parallel to the ground ("The Newlyweds of the Eiffel Tower", 1928). When a donkey walks through the sky carrying a reclining woman on its back, the earth appears above them, upside down, and forms a paradoxical, natural and terrestrial vault.

Such a universe obeys only those *rules of mirages* of which Eluard spoke in his poem dedicated to Chagall, published in 1947. The true logic is that of dreams; that of an *Oriental* art that the West considers astonishing chaos. Without knowing it, without doing it intentionally, the Orient decenters our logic, contests our principles and shakes the foundations on which we base our assurance. When Chagall met the actor Wachtangoff, he said, "We looked at each other awkwardly. There was no doubt: he read in my eyes the chaos and disorder of the Orient, an incomprehensible, foreign art."

THE SONG OF IGNORANCE

This disorder has no literary basis: very rightly, he shies away from symbols, literature, discourses. He has chosen ignorance, he prefers innocence to knowledge: "I wanted," he said, at the time of the inauguration of the Opéra de Paris ceiling, "to sing like a bird without theory or method." Thus, he refuses to explain his monstrous forms, the monstrous phenomena that haunt his space. In Paris, before the First World War, he said to Lounatcharsky, "Above all, don't ask me why I paint in blue or in green or why a calf can be seen in the belly of a cow." In 1947, L. Degand related remarks that confirm this refusal to explain: "And so if in a painting I cut the head off a cow, if I put the head upside down,

MARC CHAGALL. The Cock over Paris. Original lithograph. (Ed. Maeght.)

if I have sometimes worked on paintings the wrong way up, it is not to make literature. It is to give my picture a psychic shock that is always motivated by plastic reasons... If, finally, one nonetheless discovers a symbol in my picture, it was strictly unintentional on my part... I am against any sort of literature in painting."

Chagall refuses words and fables. His paintings, the monstrous forms in his paintings reject, contest all verbal interpretations, render derisive all hermeneutic efforts. On the surface of the canvas, flight, dancing and laughter are sketched in. A rapid line. A spontaneity that seeks itself without ever catching up. "A perpetual birth" says Eluard. There is nothing behind the representation, nothing under the surface. But, undoubtedly, as Gilles Deleuze proposes in his *Logique du Sens*, the conquest of surfaces is, in theory as in sensuality, the supreme effort of psychic life: "The most profound is very little".

HEBRAIC JOY

This art of surfaces is an art of happiness. The prose of the world becomes illuminated without losing its simplicity. The miracle is *daily*, both frequent and banal. The most extraordinary forms are, for Chagall, the most natural. On seeing his canvases, one thinks of the ingenuity of Hebraic tales such as M. Buber recounts them. During a moment of rapture, Baal-Shem-Tov "had not noticed that he was on the edge of a yawning abyss; and already he had one foot almost in it. With a single leap, the mountain opposite him was there, squeezing against its neighbor; and Baal-Shem passed." During a prayer by Baal-Shem, "the water of a trough, which was trembling, started quivering, boiling and making waves"; perhaps this trough was similar to that which Chagall painted in 1925, to that which constitutes his first childhood memory and of which he speaks in the first line of *My Life*. When the Rabbi of Apta died, his coffin flew to Palestine. The clothing of the Rabbi of Lublin, during one of his absences, spoke among themselves in a discreet whisper, of his greatness. Baal-Shem crossed the Dniestr twice, walking on the waters.

Everyone can see the relationship between the Hebrew world and Chagall's world. When, in *My Life*, he speaks of his father, we recognize the tone adopted by the disciples of the miraculous rabbis: "My father's clothes sometimes shone with pickle brine. Reflections fell beyond them, from above, from the sides." In his works, too, mountains leap about, objects and human beings fly, clothes become animated, God is omnipresent. The prose of the world and the transcendency, the trivality and the miracle, the sensual and the sacred are all united.

Too often, theorists identify Judaism and anxiety. Although seldom minimizing anxiety, Freud has taught us to recognize Jewish joy. For Freud, the Jew is essentially prosaic: "Ah, Emile," he wrote to E. Fluss, the 16th of June, 1873, "why are you a prosaic Jew? Certain artisans with a Germano-Christian sentimentality have, in like circumstances, composed magnificent poems." On July 23, 1882, speaking of his fiancée and of his grandfather, he mentioned the latter's theory: "The Jew is made for joy... The law encourages Jews to find pleasure in the smallest joys, to give a benediction before each fruit that recalls the bonds attaching them to the beautiful universe in which that fruit ripened. The Jew is made for joy and joy is made for the Jew."

Undoubtedly, that joy which the works of Chagall explore and diffuse is not without an element of sadness. Speaking of his viola, he describes it as "sad and joyous". However happy they may be, his monstrous forms are disquieting. They dazzle. When we see the red, thunderstruck angel in the "Fall of the Angel" (1923-33-47), we think of Rilke's words: "Any angel is terrible." Furthermore, in a dream, Chagall lived this mixture of delight and fear: "Suddenly the ceiling opens and a winged creature comes down with flashing light and noise, filling the room with movement and clouds. A rustling of dragging wings. I think: an angel! I can't open my eyes, the light is too bright, too luminous."

The houses dance, "the colors revolt," "the city seems to split in two, like the strings of a violin," lovers fly around in the sky. The omnipotence of God's desire, the violence of nature, the joy of lovers annihilate differences, abolish categories. All order is contested. A new, fascinating world never ceases to be born. A joy radiates from his works, such a joy that it is sometimes difficult to support: we run the risk of abolishing ourselves in it. Happiness constitutes a dissarrangement, a disturbance of things pushed to the limit, becoming intolerable. Joy can kill us. The delirium of the "Song of Songs" is murderous folly.

GILBERT LASCAULT

The Unicorn. Watercolor. 14 x 10½ in. Charles Sorlier Coll., Paris.

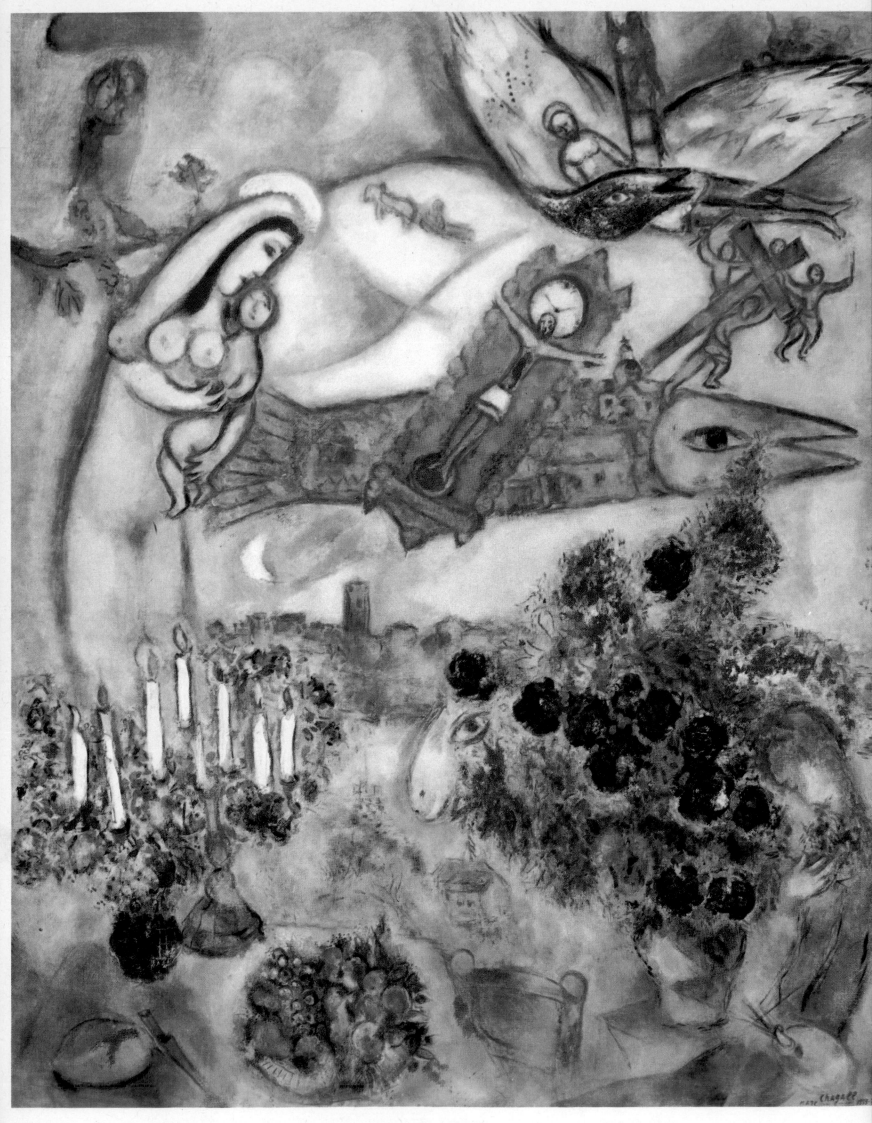

MARC CHAGALL. In the neighborhood of Vence. Oil. 1957. Maeght Fondation, Saint Paul de Vence.

Marc Chagall
lover of the Mediterranean

by André Verdet

Marc Chagall and his wife Vava, receiving André Verdet in their drawing-room.

Exiled in the United States since June 1941, Marc Chagall returned permanently to France in 1948, after a short visit in 1947.

Once back in France, the artist, in his grave happiness at living again in his adopted country, nevertheless, desired calm and an existence away from large cities, not to forget but the better to recapture his inner life. Orgeval, near Saint-Germain, welcomed him. A rustic atmosphere was noticeable in his compositions of flowers and landscapes. The town's church steeple is found in his canvases, like the one in his distant and sacrificed Vitebsk—just as in the future he was to paint the steeples of Saint Jeannet, Vence and Saint Paul.

In Orgeval, Marc Chagall, while painting "Night in Orgeval", remembered nostalgically southern France and Upper Provence, Gordes, near Apt. He remembered the old house he had lived in during the first months of the Occupation of France and even before, in more distant times, the wooded landscapes of the Alps near Nice, in Peira Cava (visits between 1925 and 1930). There was a longing within him, a tenacious longing for light and azure space. This longing was soon to become hope.

The artist explored the ground, so to speak, before a final decision by visiting in 1949, Saint Jean Cap Ferrat near his friend Teriade, the publisher, and then another visit to Saint Jeannet, near Vence. Work on gouaches and tinted drawings filled in the hours after walks through the region. In Vence, finally, he rented a villa and a

short time afterwards he decided on his Mediterranean destiny by buying the white dwelling belonging to Claude and Ida Bourdet, "Les Collines", situated on the side of a wooded hill with a valley nearby.

Meridional nature subjugates Chagall. The light there has not only a secret sensitivity but also intelligence. The painter found the same "occupied" space that he had known before in Gordes. Little by little he took root in the sunny climate. The arts of the earth and the kiln attracted him. The ceramics that he made and decorated in the Ateliers Madonna in Vallauris are a transposition in sculptured and colored form of his paintings. The same legendary colors, the same plentiful pigmentation lighten them, transporting them in the space of a weightless dream.

Marc Chagall then rented a large studio in a painter's home to create vast panels concerning a powerfully spiritual theme, a theme that was beginning to awake in him, to uplift him with a secret fervor, to fill him with a grace both wild and appeasing: "The Biblical Message". It was the ideal vision of votive chapels of the Stations of the Cross in Vence that gave him this inspiration. A sort of intoxication griped him, like whiffs of perfume—"A real emotional shock," Chagall said later.

For a long period of happiness, the artist married Valentine Brodsky, "Vava" for close friends, with her grave and matte face like those in icons, who, bringing harmony and peace, was to spare him a maximum of daily constraints in life. Vava

then had built at "Les Collines" a large studio for the preparation of "The Biblical Message", a work that proved difficult because he gave himself to it both physically and morally to the point of a sort of painful joy in its accomplishment. However, the work of painting "The Biblical Message" also gave him comfort and a certitude that rejuvenated him in body and soul.

The measurements of the pictures are in proportion to the size of chapels. An immediate understanding was established between the initial image and its psycho-pictorial realization. Not a single profane picture was included that would have broken the spiritual unity of "The Biblical Message", a work that Marc Chagall has since given to the city of Nice and which will decorate the galleries of a lovely building built expressly for this purpose on one of the hills of Nice, in Cimiez.

The Mediterranean Chagall grew more profound after his trips to Israel and Greece in 1951 and 1954. Furthermore, Teriade asked him to illustrate Daphnis et Chloe. The years in Vence were as fruitful as those of Saint Paul were later to be, intense in the solitude of a garden filled with the humming of insects and the songs of birds where, in good weather, he could set up his canvases under the trees and near flower beds "to see if they could stand the test, to see if they were truly the fluidic continuation of nature and not a lie about it."

Unforgettable paintings were born in the studios in Vence and grew without haste, each painting being for Chagall a whole life and not just a

ing to a dazzling and grave existence beyond joy and pain.

Still in Vence, Chagall was commissioned by the Frankfurt Theater to create the "Comedia dell'Arte", a mural painting in which musical instruments, the crowd, tight-rope walkers and animals blend together and live in a fanfare of light.

Life went on, calmly and profoundly, with visits to Paris and abroad. Drives and walks with Vava in the backcountry, on the lunar plateaux of the Vence Ridge or of Coursegoules, where some rocks resemble priests or sentries, sometimes occupied his afternoons. He was seldom seen in the streets of Vence although his silhouette was, nonetheless, familiar and neighbor_ hood bookstores sent him many albums to sign. For Vence he drew one of his most beautiful posters and the city made him an honorary citizen. Every day that rose or drew to an end brought him its cargo of daydreams, of fantasies or of poetic ecstasy, of fabulous tales: the whole irrational universe of the marvelous in which Chagall has created his own myths, his own pictorial cosmogony. The nostalgia for an else-where of innocence and love has continued to radiate from his canvases but this nostalgia is transmuted into a fresh gladness that transports forms and colors.

Sometimes anxiety and uneasiness came back to the surface and at such times he painted dramatic pictures such as the "Exodus" (1952-1956), and "War" (1952-1956), which correspond to "The Flayed Ox". Then with his composition of flowers and still-lifes that he had rediscovered with more keenness and vision because of his contact with the Côte d'Azur, he recaptured serenity in spite of an underlying anxiety.

Marc Chagall tries to merit the good fortune he has to live by the Mediterranean, on the shores of that civilizing sea, haunted by antique myths that are not completely dead because the ashes of the vanished gods are still so tenacious, because that sea and that azure land are so propitious for a more ample revelation of inner life.

Under the southern sky a bouquet of flowers looks different from one in Paris, a face or a landscape different from those in Vitebsk or New York. Imperceptibly Chagall's painting, under the influence of his environment, has undergone a change, as if from within: a molecular shift, minute new elements in the basic composition of his pictorial chemistry. It cannot be seen directly but must be sought out; it is a sort of radiation. Nonetheless, it is easy to see that certain canvases of the Vence period, or later the Saint Paul period, belong to a time of graphic supremacy and that their chromatism becomes more airy in spatial light: for example, "The Yellow Sun" (1958), or "The Large Nude with a Basket" (1955). The blues especially—and Cha-

portion of one, ripened for a long period in the plenitude of human sentiment.

Marc Chagall has abandoned Paris but returned in 1952, not forgetting the city that formerly welcomed him, nor what he owes it which he proved by a long series of paintings devoted to Paris.

"The Dance", "The Circus" (1951), "The Crossing of the Red Sea" (1952), "Night in Vence" (1952-1956), "The Concert" (1954-1957), "The Lady Rooster" (1956-1960)—such are the titles, among others, of already famous paintings that were born in Vence. It was also during that period that the series of lithographs of "The Circus" and "The Bible" were completed. Between 1960 and 1962 he composed the vast mural panel "My Life", the most important work in the Chagall gallery in the Maeght Foundation, where the artist's obsessive themes are assembled in an almost panoramic totality, and form an enchanted fresco, an immense bouquet of love, a triumphant offer-

In front of the mosaic of his house.

gall's are the most beautiful in the world—take on a deep limpidity, a more atmospheric, nocturnal sparkle. I am thinking of those that cast a magic spell on the canvases, such as "The Lady Rooster" (1956-1960), "Repose" (1966), or "The Flying Fish" (1966). Chagall's sensitivity to tones is great; the artist catches what is essential around him and then stores it. When it is rendered, in the face of mute interrogations, it is only bit by bit and then, one day, a totality appears pictorially, adapting itself to the mental landscape which is not only the mirror of past experiences viewed in the present, but also the mirror of past acquisitions: a transformation, a transposition has taken place with a secret slowness, from one change to another, as in nature itself.

It will only be in a few decades that we will be able to grasp with certainty the influence of the Mediterranean region on Chagall's work because each of his works requires time to ripen, to express it's entity which is both psychological and plastic; that is, its final revelation.

Now Marc Chagall has left Vence for Saint Paul. Although he was very happy at "Les Collines" and his relationship with the city of Vence was excellent, the construction of a five-storied building opposite his house, on the near horizon of his view, created a condition unbearable for his need of harmony. "My usual landscape was mutilated. I was sick at heart. It was distressing!"

Sensing Marc's growing sadness, Vava looked for land on which to build a new house where

there would be no danger of one day seeing cranes and beams rising in front of them. She found it in the Gardelles woods in the Saint Paul municipality amidst green oaks and pines, facing west and the mountains of Esterel and not far from the Maeght Foundation. Vava immediately had work started on the construction of the new house.

The couple have lived in this sunny, restful and healthy refuge since July 1966. It is a house, built with regional stone, especially conceived for work, relaxation and the pleasure of light and that avoids the fatigue of going from one room to another. It is called "La Colline" in memory of their home in Vence. There are few flowers in the garden but many in the vases in the large livingroom. A lawn stretches out in front of the house with gleaming olive trees on it—trees very dear to the painter and somewhat like the presence of a wish fulfilled. On an angle of a wall a mosaic is incrusted: "The Great Sun", an offering from the painter to his wife.

Three studios form the east wing of the house. One is intended for engraving work and the two others for painting. The larger of the two has a mobile wall, arranged in such a way that the artist is not obliged to climb up on a scaffolding for the composition of vast panels.

Happy and lively, with witty eyes in a face that, strangely, has retained its youthfulness, Marc Chagall does not show his eighty-three years. To take a rest from his work, he often walks in his wooded park, along forest paths and roads that

abound near his home and his faun-like face quickens when he encounters a sylvan fragrance during his solitary walks.

The few years already spent in Saint-Paul have proved to be benefic for this artist whose love of work is so strong that it regulates his life and determines his hours. From the studios of "La Colline" have come the models for the synagogue of Jerusalem, the Zurich cathedral, the Metz cathedral and for the Rockfeller chapel; the models for the ceiling of the Opéra, for the stage setting of Mozart's Enchanted Flute, *for the "Ulysses" mosaic in the School of Fine Arts in Nice, and countless other works. Naming pell-mell some of the paintings conceived in Saint Paul since 1966 that have already attracted our attention are "The Horseman", "Winter", "The Mauve Nude", "The Descent from the Cross" and "Easter" in black and white.*

The medieval city of Saint Paul which, in spite of the invasion of tourists, nas been able to safeguard its enchanting qualities, has not effaced in Chagall's heart the memory of his native Vitebsk. This corner of Mediterranean earth has blended with the memory of a faraway corner of Slav earth. It is in the twilight of his years, in the sunny peacefulness of Saint Paul, that the exiled painter recaptures the most easily his childhood land and, although giving thanks to the welcoming Mediterranean, he continues to show Vitebsk the gratitude of an inspired son—and that gratitude is a universal song.

ANDRÉ VERDET

Marc Chagall's sculptures and ceramics

by Jacques Thirion
Curator of the National Museums of France

Marc Chagall's paintings, stained-glass windows and engravings have provoked countless warm commentaries, but there is an aspect of his work, so rich and so fascinating, that is much less known and that should be studied more often; that is, his ceramics and sculptures.

There is no question in these few pages of going to the heart of the subject—which will soon appear in book form—but simply to draw attention to its value.

This part of Chagall's work is relatively recent.

Furthermore, it is the object of the artist's jealous care and most of it has remained in his studio.

Of course, everyone knows the large ceramic panel, *The Crossing of the Red Sea*, created in 1957 for the baptistery of the Assy church; we have also seen in several art exhibitions tiles, plates, vases, pots, especially in Maeght's Gallery in 1950 (La Fontaine's *Fables*) and 1957, and in Curt Vallentin's New York Gallery in 1952, in Palazzo Madama in Turin in 1953, in the Kunsthalle of Basel and Bern in 1956, and in the

MARC CHAGALL. The Donkey. Sculpture. Height: 20⁷/₈ in, Length: 27½ in. (Photo Delagenière).

Stedelijk Museum of Amsterdam in 1956. However, these were only a matter of a few show-cases grouped with an exhibition of paintings. The first exhibition devoted especially to ceramics—organized at Madoura's in Cannes in 1962—although it too was very limited, has nonetheless allowed us to get an over-all impression. As for his sculptures, of which only a few have been shown, they are even less known.

Chagall's research in the field of the kiln arts coincided—and this is significant—with his settling in Provence in the old city of Vence in 1950. In this country, near Greece and the Promised Land, privileged by its light, the austere majesty of its landscapes, its leafy vegetation, its fields with silvery olive trees, the blue horizon of the sea, the artist who is a poet, attentive to everything that covers the earth and populates the sky, even the humblest creatures, found, more than elsewhere, the beauty, even the sacred character, of one of the oldest and most rustic arts: that of

the potter. It is there that he became fully conscious of its necessity. "In Provence," Chagall said, "the earth burns your fingers." The renown of Vallauris, made famous by Picasso, also rang in his ears. Chagall, always curious about techniques—he also worked at the same time on stained-glass windows and tapestries—feels that the ceramic art can only be approached successfully in an age of maturity and synthesis. We know the importance he attributes to what he calls "the chemistry" of painting. Ceramic work requires, from a technical point of view, special care. With the baking, waiting, drying, coats of varnish, it imposes constraints on the hand as well as the mind. The artist can be victorious only if he is in full possession of his capabilities. It is good, the perpetually uneasy Chagall believes, that these new servitudes work as an antidote for the temptation of facility to which every artist in his zenith is prey. Finally, for him, sculpture and ceramics are not mere diversions nor simple exercises to keep the painter "in form". It is the flowering of his art.

MARC CHAGALL. Couple with a Goat. Height: 8½ x 14¾ in. (Photo Delagenière).

MARC CHAGALL. Ceramic.

MARC CHAGALL. The Blue Donkey. Ceramic.

Indeed, there is not the slightest breach between Chagall's paintings and his ceramics. The latter are only a prolongation of the former. They realize them perfectly. Gifted with the third dimension, they will live, henceforth, in space and are enriched, thanks to the caprices of the kiln, by new tactile attractions. They give us a desire to touch them, to caress them.

I will leave aside here the ceramic tiles which, in groups, form more or less large pictures, as well as the platters and plates, often oval and scarcely concave, on which are reflected paintings as if in heavy mirrors, to speak mostly about his small and large vases, jugs, and pots.

Chagall began his ceramic experiences in a pottery works in Antibes in 1950, with a series of plates illustrating the *Fables* of La Fontaine that were exhibited shortly thereafter in Maeght's Gallery. Then he made a large, hand-sculptured vase for his daughter Ida, incrusted plates, very

MARC CHAGALL. Woman in Her Bath. Sculpture. Height: 14⅛ in.

MARC CHAGALL. Crucifixion. Stone. H. 31¹/₅ in L. 12 ft 6 in.

pale in color, with Biblical subjects, (they fill a marvelous glass cabinet in his villa in Vence), painted tiles for the decoration of Assy, and many pots, using the kilns of various pottery works in Antibes, Vence, Biot, Valbonnes, and Vallauris. The most recent vases were created in 1962, in Vallauris in Madame Ramier's studio. For each of his works Chagall made several precise drawings, using colored pencils to determine the harmony of color and the rhythm of each object of which only one example was made. One can well imagine with what care he watched over its manufacture.

Chagall's ceramics are extremely original, both in form and color. From the point of view of form, one can distinguish two groups: simple vases with traditional lines; and pitchers, pots and vases where the artist gave free rein to his imagination.

For the vases, Chagall was content to make the most of their rounded sides, with marvelous ease and skill, enlivening them with undulating and fluid compositions that give the whole a pleasant gyratory movement. The viewer has the impression that the vase is going to revolve; he cannot resist walking around it in order to follow the dreamlike figures that curve around the sides: languid naiads with pearly bodies: moonlight reflected on marine currents of subtle shadings, clear or golden, azure or emerald; delicate bouquets of flowers—roses or mimosa—inhabited by fabulous birds whose gentle songs of love seem to hypnotize, long, nostalgic profiles in a summer sky on the *Vase with a Mermaid and Face* (1962. H. 13";). Occasionally there is a more slender vase with a high neck to make room for figures of more affected gracefulness. Examples of this form are *The Woman with the Blue Donkey* (1962. H. 16"; W. 8¹/₄"), where, in a balmy Oriental night, a donkey with a muzzle as caressing as a kiss watches over a woman in love, lost in her dreams. In these delicate works, all treated with nuances, the forms are sometimes underlined by hollowed out lines.

The pots and pitchers, by their exuberance, are different from the modest forms of the vases: here, the abundance of handles and spouts has nothing to do with utility; these outgrowths are, above all, a prolongation of themes which thus find a tumultuous and chatoyant development. They rise, overflow, bend like a statue: some of these ceramics are veritable sculptures, such as *The Rooster* (1954. H. 18¹/₂"; W. 16¹/₄"). But they also stand out by the delicacy of their colors, their generally light harmonies, their tender, mat surfaces, as fragile and precious as Mycenaean potteries. This soft, velvety aspect is the result of the artist's most recent research. Nothing could be more different from the shiny varnish, often a little vulgar, of most contemporary ceramic

MARC CHAGALL. Two Heads. Marble. Height: 15¼ in.

127

works. Instead of reflecting exterior light, Chagall's potteries seem, to the contrary, to absorb it or, rather, their phosphorescent colors seem to spring from the clay itself under the effect of some mysterious transpiring, due to the magic of dark light. They are illuminated from within just as his paintings transmit the image of an interior reality, the poet's own, and the reality that surrounds us.

In the very special universe of his studio, Chagall's ceramics are very naturally impregnated with his familiar myths, a little bit as the color of flora in the ocean depths leaves its mark on nearby amphorae and shells. His vases reveal the majority of subjects that the Master of Vitebsk never tires of reinventing: *The Blue Donkey* (1954. H. 11⅜"; W. 8⅜"), tenderly ironic as in the fable, serves as a figure-head, with its luminous coloration—for a pitcher of rustic inspiration—ochre, brown, dark green, black—on the sides of which,

MARC CHAGALL. Sculptured vase. 1954. Height: 17¾ in. (Photo Delagenière).

MARC CHAGALL. The Cock. 1954. Height: 18½ in, Length: 16⅛ in.

blithely, dance houses in a village with its rooster and tender lovers.

The Peasant at the Well (1954. H. 12³/₄″; W. 9¹/₂″) with its cheerful, pale yellow harmony—symbol of Provençal light—brightened by pale blue, green, brown and black—celebrates just as naïvely the happiness of country life. It depicts a peasant in a firm stance serving as a spout, next to the familiar view of Vence, the "new Vitebsk", where

Chagall has found, after torment, "the heartbreaking joy of living." Vence is also profiled on the other side of *Two Women* (1957. H. 12¹/₂″) who are smiling at each other, holding a bouquet in a graceful movement that is closer to sculpture than to the potter's art. It is significant that these pitchers tell a story on each side. On the other side of *Two Women*, an hallucinating crucifixion floats in the sky while a donkey drinks

129

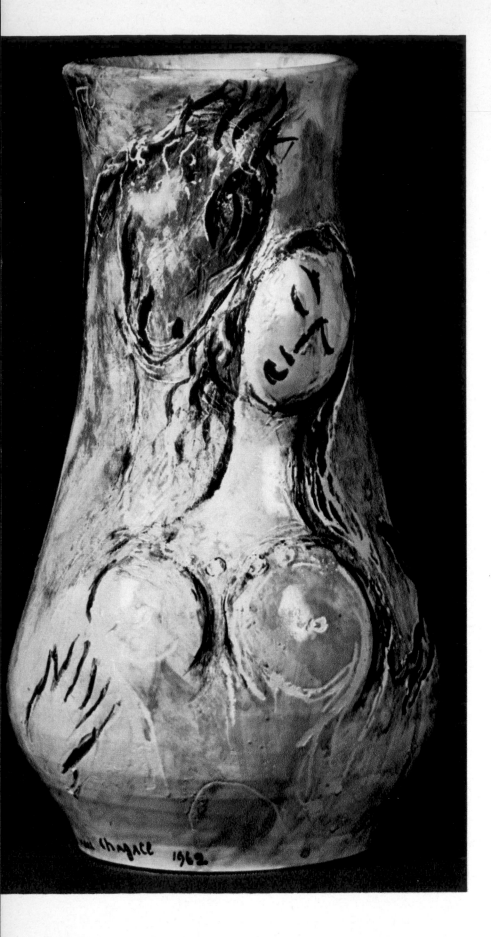

under a very definitely malefic moon. The colors themselves—red, ochre, blue-gray, black set off by white—illuminate these figures with their tragic gleam. The *Two Heads* (1957. H. 12¹/₂″), glowing from beautiful red clay, enhanced by dashes of white, black, yellow and green, are even more extraordinary: they exalt Provence, of course, but are also disturbing memories of Russia with the intoxicated village bristling with bulbar towers and their two resigned faces overlooked by a comical and melancholy donkey. As for the decorated *Sculptured Vase* (1954. H. 17³/₄″), in a very "baked" reddish paste, of a feminine figure, as fascinating as a Cretan idol, it is almost more a sculpture than a vase. The same is true of the *Rooster* (1954. H. 18¹/₂″; W. 16″), as fantastic as a Ming bronze. Its very pale paste is tatooed with a pair of lovers sketched in bister with a light touch.

In order better to understand the continuity that exists between Chagall's paintings and ceramics, it would be tempting to compare a number of them with such and such a painting or gouache but that would carry us too far afield.

These ceramics appear to be gorged with all of his myths, like beautiful cacti or wild flowers, blooming freely in the southern sun of France. They have been liberated from the constraints of traditional forms. Nothing could distress Chagall more than to call them "decorative art", and he would not be wrong for they owe nothing to stylization. How different they are from the decorative research, the nervous but strict graphism, the somewhat convulsed figures of the ceramics signed by Picasso, Cocteau, Lurçat or the "abstract" designs of Miró.

Once again, the master of Vence wins by simply singing of his love of life, his marvel over flowers, birds, stars, or his memories and dreams.

Thus, his art remains in contact with nature and participates both by its miraculous liberty and order. This is what Chagall calls "to continue life". He dreams of an art that would be the very vital impulse of life, like that of the human song or that of the bird, like the blooming of a flower. "Art cannot be made with theories," he added. "Painting and ceramics are made with the hands and the heart. Theories come after the work. They arise from the latter, they are not the source." Chagall is perfectly willing that his potteries be decorative but in the same way as the ancient Chinese and Japanese porcelains or Greek vases are, "which have a stylized appearance," he says, "but whose lines are, in reality, miraculously free, for they, too, express the rhythm of life."

In Provence, not only the earth "burns the fingers". There is also the stone, as polished as marble, and all sorts of smooth, flat rocks. Cha-

MARC CHAGALL. Woman on a Blue Donkey. Height: 15¾ in. Width: 8¼ in.

MARC CHAGALL. Two Women. Jug. 1957. Height: 12⅜ in. (Photo Delagenière).

Among the most striking, let us mention *The Couple with the Goat* (H. 8¹/₂″; W. 14³/₄″), a charming image of a juvenile embrace, with supple arabesques, sheltered by foliage and flowers, and with the sole complicity of the moon and a tender young goat—or the *Two Heads* (H. 15¹/₄″), this time detached from the base and which is one of the purest, tenderest and most spell-casting representations of the kiss that has ever been sculptured. What reserve and what intensity in their longing for each other, in that mute complicity protected by a caressing hand!

Chagall loves his neighbor but he also loves himself, which is very natural, and his wife Valentine at the same time. Thus, he depicted himself humorously, accompanied by a redeeming feminine silhouette in an amazing chiselled medallion (Diam. 14¹/₂″), its style reminiscent of Gauguin with the subtle lines and majesty of an Aztec emperor.

But Chagall's most astonishing sculptures are, without a doubt, his terra cottas and his bronzes cast by Susse in very small quantities. Capturing the third dimension, they are an autonomous reality and no longer a complementary transposition.

The Donkey (H. 21″; W. 27¹/₂″), a demoniac animal in this case, with its troubling profile, a vehicle in its flanks and a limping walk, is a haunting figuration of the couple.

The Mother Holding Her Child (H. 26¹/₂″) carries him to her bosom in a wide gesture, a symbol of pride and protection, her face proud and anxious at the same time. She evokes by her buxomness the blooming of the robust divinities of the art of Aurignac. *The Bathing Woman* (H. 14¹/₄″) recalls the vigor of the vineyardists of Roman art who also splashed in their vats (how can one not think of the wine-harvesters on the Autun tympanum?), with its gyration accentuated by the circular tub from which she emerges, her beautiful, inflected torso, broad, granular, and seeming to shine with soap. It is one of the most striking bathers in contemporary sculpture.

The simplicity, the frankness, the power of these sculptures merit reflection. They are a flat contradiction to all those who would like to consider Chagall as a colorist only. If he makes objects fly about, if he envelopes them in colored vibrations according to his reveries, he nevertheless possesses a very sure instinct for construction. Nature is liberty but it is also harmony. Movement should not be confused with gravity. The Ferris wheel in a country fair turns and creates an impression of vertigo: it is nonetheless solidly built. The purified images that Chagall's sculptures offer are admirable proof of his vitality and equilibrium.

JACQUES THIRION

gall, who feels almost physically the call of this antique country, has found on its soil the emotions he experienced during his voyage to Greece in 1952, during which he admired the archaic statuary of the Museum of Athens and the sculptures of Olympia. For this reason, he feverishly began to sculpture between 1952 and 1958. He first sculptured, at the request of Father Couturier, using themes from verses of the Psalms, small bas-reliefs in marble for the Assy baptistry. Then he made small statues in marble that are clarified transpositions. They remind one, more than of archaic Greece, of the spontaneity and enigmatic power of the first Roman age. They are inspired by his familiar themes, in particular the couple: *The Couple and the Bird* (H. 12¹/₄″; W. 12¹/₂″). *La Vague à l'Ane or Lovers* (H. 8¹/₂″; W. 15³/₄″, a two-sided sculpture).

HOMAGE TO MARC CHAGALL

AN ORIGINAL COLOR LITHOGRAPH BY MARC CHAGALL.

Editorial assistant: Sophie Pompidou.

Translations by:
Mrs Jacques FERMAUD, Joyce REEVES, Noel BURCH.

© by XXᵉ siècle, Paris. Printed in Italy by Amilcare Pizzi S.p.A., Milan.

TUDOR PUBLISHING CO. NEW YORK.